CONTENTS

ROBERT LEPAGE
CONNECTING FLIGHTS

ROBERT LEPAGE CONNECTING FLIGHTS

RÉMY CHAREST

Translated from the French by Wanda Romer Taylor

METHUEN

Published by Methuen

First published as *Quelques zones de liberté* in 1995 by
Editions de L'instant même, Québec

Cover photograph by Bengt Wanselius
Other photographs by Véro Boncompagni, Michael Cooper, Armando Gallo, Claudel
Huot, François Lachapelle, Daniel Mallard, Emmanuel Valette, Bengt Wanselius
reproduced by kind permission

First published in the United Kingdom in 1997 by Methuen,
Random House, 20 Vauxhall Bridge Road, London SW1V 2SA

Random House Australia (Pty) Limited
20 Alfred Street, Milsons Point, Sydney,
New South Wales 2061, Australia

Random House New Zealand Limited
18 Poland Road, Glenfield
Auckland 10, New Zealand

Random House South Africa (Pty) Limited
Endulini, 5A Jubilee Road, Parktown 2193, South Africa

Random House UK Limited Reg. No. 954009

A CIP catalogue rocord for this book
is available fom the British Library

ISBN 0413 70690 7

Typeset in Bembo by MATS, Southend-on-Sea, Essex
Printed and bound in Great Britain by Mackays of Chatham PLC

BEGINNING

ACKNOWLEDGEMENTS

It is not surprising that a book of interviews such as this is a distilling of much dialogue and discussion. The extent to which this has been a process of continuous exchange between Robert Lepage and me, however, was beyond what I expected. All the people mentioned here (some of whom I am surely forgetting) have been, to a certain extent, partners in the project as well.

Robert Lepage, of course, is the first one to thank. Throughout the interviews and the writing of the book (1994–5), he made himself completely available and turned this work – like everything he touches – into a collaborative effort. The editors of the French edition, Gilles Pellerin and Marie Taillon, of Quebec City's L'Instant même, provided encouragement and many enlightening comments on the form of the book. For the English translation, the dialogue continued with Wanda Romer Taylor, who helped me clarify what I had originally written.

Many people close to Robert Lepage helped me in various ways: the ever patient and insightful Michel Bernatchez, the indispensable Marie Gignac, the vigilant Jean-Pierre Saint-Michel, as well as Robert Thuot, Philippe Soldevila, and Diane Bastin. On the London front, Michael Morris and everyone else at Cultural Industry also have my gratitude for their constant attention, advice and sympathy. *Tack så mycket* also to Peder

Bjurman and everyone at Stockholm's Kungliga Dramatiska Teatern for welcoming me in the fall of 1994, when the work on this book truly began.

Last but not least, I also give heartfelt thanks to my own circle of readers, commentators and supporters: my parents, Louise MacDonald and Michel Charest, my good friends Elaine Normandeau and Vincent Desautels, as well as my wonderful wife Geneviève Ribordy. I would like to dedicate this book to her, and to Mathilde, our latest creative endeavour.

TRANSLATOR'S NOTE

My challenge with this translation was not only to reproduce Robert Lepage's voice in English, but also (despite the fixed nature of the text itself) to suggest the fluidity and perpetual evolution of his creative mind. Lepage's drive to explore the anarchic depths of the human soul and willingness to reveal his own self in the process are inspiring to all artists. It was a wonderful privilege to have lived in the fertile chaos of his imagination over the past several months.

I would like to express my sincere gratitude to Paul Keenan and Craig Walker for their helpful comments and suggestions. Victoria Hipps's and Sabine Jaccaud's skilful copy-editing of the final draft is also gratefully acknowledged. Finally, a special thank you to Rémy Charest for his highly intelligent editing of the text, his sensitivity to and love for the word (in both languages) and his good-natured support through trying moments.

INTRODUCTION TO THE ENGLISH EDITION

It has been my experience that Robert Lepage's work, whether for theatre, opera, cinema or rock concerts, often leads to a three-step reaction in people who see it. When first confronted by it, spectators are stunned and amazed by the formal invention, the unique story-telling, the striking images and a certain sense of playfulness. So much so that the programme notes for the presentation of the solo show *Needles and Opium* at the Tokyo Globe Theatre mentioned that it was impossible to know what the shows looked like from the press clippings, because they read like reports of an almost mystical experience.

After seeing a few productions, the element of surprise largely wears off, leading many to wonder if they were not just seduced by a remarkable capacity for razzle-dazzle, magical tricks and acrobatic moves. With Lepage's unique capacity to draw forth strong images on stage and screen, to make the seemingly impossible happen, it is somewhat inevitable that there would first be the excitement of novelty and that this excitement would tend to wear off.

Fortunately, most audiences come back to see more of his shows despite this slight drop in adrenalin levels, leading to a third phase where discussion replaces adulation, where the metaphoric and poetic qualities of Robert Lepage's and his collaborators' work, as well as the deeper reasons for their formal preoccupations and for the presence of certain recurrent themes, begin to appear more clearly. Then the pleasure of still being surprised at times combines with a more informed perception of his work.

Like many other people around the world, my first-step reaction came from seeing *The Dragons' Trilogy* in the spring of 1987, at a time when my interest in theatre was beginning to take shape. As a young man barely out of high school, I could hardly afford to pay to see a play twice, yet I came back to see this one, and dragged my parents along (they might have helped with the price of the ticket, mind you). I even brought a notebook, in order to write down my impressions of the play, and to try to make some sense of the overwhelming emotion which had overcome me initially. Now, if you had recently asked me what my impressions of the play had been at the time, I would have talked of stunning images; of the moving musical score by Robert Caux; of the great cast of characters; of the theatrical sleight of hand which transformed a parking attendant's booth into a stairwell to a dark basement; of the funny way in which two actresses playing little girls used shoeboxes to recreate a whole neighbourhood of Quebec City; of the general capacity to transform the rectangular sand-pit which was the set into so many parts of the world.

As I began writing these lines, I decided to look for the notes I had taken almost ten years ago. Much to my surprise, I discovered something quite different in the words I had laboured to scribble legibly in pitch darkness. What I found was a transcription of the mythical opening and closing lines of the show, some lovely pieces of dialogue, notes on the connections between characters and, especially, several comments on the use of shoes.

In *The Dragons' Trilogy*, shoes were a powerful resource for story-telling. A pair was taken out of a suitcase to show a child's first steps, and then bigger and bigger shoes showed the child's growth. Another pair was put into a suitcase to signify a mother's death. Shoes were also carefully lined up all along the set by another character, only to be trampled by soldiers walking on ice skates – an unusual but most powerful evocation of the Second World War's destruction. Thus, the most modest of stage props, the most common objects of daily life were used to show birth, life and death, the love of a father and mother and the hideous devastation of war. The deepest and most important potential of the theatre was there: putting all the world onto a stage.

In other words, what had struck me most weren't stunning images or great scenes – striking though they were – but something which lies at the very heart of theatre: transformation and connections. This seems like good news to me: the astonishment of the first-step reaction may not be far at all from the deeper understanding that can later come as the relationship between the audience and the work develops. Also, it tells me once again that, with Robert Lepage, the way you see things at first glance certainly doesn't give you a complete picture of what's going on – so much so that a play may lead you to feel one thing while actually thinking another, both initially and over a long period of time.

At the time of my first encounter with *The Dragons' Trilogy*, the three-hour version of this collective work was being shown in Quebec City, only a few weeks before the fully developed, six-hour play was to begin taking the world by storm during a tour which lasted until the end of 1991. In the few years before this creation came to life, Lepage had become one of the hottest directors in Quebec: *Circulations*, created in 1984 with composer Bernard Bonnier, had won first prize in Quebec City's International Theatre Festival and gone on to a triumphant tour of Canada where, while visiting various Chinatowns, Lepage had gathered the basic ideas for the *Trilogy*. Now, with this epic collective work and his first solo show, *Vinci*, the director would begin to go around the world, playing to packed houses and winning rave reviews at every turn, from the Festival d'Avignon to Adelaide, Australia. Suddenly, everything was going his way. Quite a change of pace for someone who hardly even knew about theatre before his teenage years.

★   ★   ★

Born in 1957 in Quebec City to a working-class French-Canadian family, which had already adopted two English-Canadian children, Robert Lepage was barely twenty years old when he began to work professionally in theatre, after graduating from the local Conservatoire d'art dramatique. In the beginning, the man who is now the Quebec director best known around the world could hardly find work. His teachers had often seen him as a sort of Jack-of-all-trades, who wasn't really good at anything specific. When he graduated, he simply didn't seem to fit in any category – so he created his own.

With his creative use of transformation staging – which was in part a necessity caused by shoestring budgets – and his preference for collaborative works, Robert Lepage gradually began to attract people's attention, and within a few years he had already begun to work on several projects at once, a work habit which has now become something of a way of life. He gained popularity with some light comedies and by playing a popular form of improvisational games. He also put on his first Shakespeare plays, worked with a puppet theatre as actor and director, participated in a number of collective creations, adapting George Orwell or Woody Allen or exploring the wonderful world of tabloid newspapers, and dabbled in opera. In 1982, he became associated with Théâtre Repère – which was to be his 'home base' for almost ten years. He scored one of his first hits with a show called *En attendant*, created with his friend and partner Richard Fréchette and Repère director Jacques Lessard.

The *Trilogy* was to be the highpoint of Robert Lepage's association with Théâtre Repère, just before his career took on a whole new direction around 1989. His productions were becoming international business. No longer limited to Quebec City, he directed the première of his next collaborative work, *Tectonic Plates*, in Toronto, at the request of producers in Glasgow and London. Meanwhile, at home in Quebec, Lepage was meeting with remarkable public success, but also with controversy and mixed reviews from the press and media. Success was becoming a little bittersweet for him.

This is in part what brought him to Ottawa in 1989, to be director of the National Arts Centre's French Theatre, a position he held for four years, during which he also spent so much time around the world that he temporarily lost resident status in Quebec. Though Canada's national capital, Ottawa was also more quiet and removed from the media hubbub of such metropolitan centres as Montreal and Toronto – for people in the arts, if not for politicians. It was there, away from our hometown, that we first met, thanks to a city where a beginner in journalism such as I could have regular interviews and even go out for lunch with Lepage, despite his overwhelming schedule.

It wasn't just the city, however. The man's character, his genuine openness, also brought about this contact. What struck me in my early meetings with him was the way in which talking about international tours and creative conundrums felt as easy as discussing the latest ball game or catching up on family news. Robert Lepage has a remarkable way of making complex ideas seem simple, of explaining things which at first feel foreign, so that they appear perfectly clear and accessible. He evidently wasn't the near mythical figure being shaped by the media. He had none of the airs of the show business 'star' that one might have naïvely expected him to have. And the work he described, the way he saw his métier, didn't correspond to others' descriptions of him. This certainly had to be told, I felt. For a good while, however, before we both came back to live and work in Quebec City, we had other fish to fry.

It was two years later that a conversation with my wife gave rise to an idea: how about a book of interviews with Robert Lepage? In early 1994, at the very first public rehearsal of the director's most ambitious collective project, *The Seven Streams of the River Ota*, I managed to get hold of Robert – often, even this can be a bit of an achievement – and talk to him about this. I remember saying to him that it felt as if it were the right time for such a project, that circumstances made it appropriate for him to reflect upon both his work and his career more extensively. He readily agreed: this new piece, set to develop over three years, was just starting, and was to be the very first project realised under Lepage's new company, Ex Machina, which was developing plans for a multimedia production centre in Quebec City, La Caserne, the construction of which was finally completed in the spring of 1997. In many ways, this was a turning point. A perfect moment to go over more than fifteen years of work, and ponder what the future might hold.

From the outset, Robert Lepage and I had agreed that this book would in no way be an attempt at a biography, nor a book of interviews in the more classical sense (i.e. a series of questions and answers set in chronological order). For a creator who hasn't even reached the age of forty, it seemed a little early to get into such 'monument building', which, in any case, his modesty precluded. The point of the operation – which was to be largely done at 'one sit-ting' in the autumn of 1994 in Stockholm, where Lepage was directing August Strindberg's *Ett Drömspel* (*A Dream Play*) – was to generate a 'travel log' of sorts, a portrait of a certain period in this artist's career.

Looking into such diverse sources as German director Ray Müller's multifaceted documentary *The Wonderful, Horrible Life of Leni Riefenstahl*, Wim Wenders's collection of essays *The Logic of Images* and a peculiar book of reflec-tions on photographs by French writer Michel Tournier, we sought to let our work guide us, to let the form and direction of our book emerge as we went along. Just like the rest of Lepage's work always does. When I came to Stockholm, the lists of subjects and themes which I had drawn from my own research, or from the insightful com-ments of longtime Lepage collaborators such as Marie Gignac, Michel Bernatchez or Philippe Soldevila, became a mere canvas on which, as often happens in works where Lepage is involved, we largely improvised and built upon.

Much like his work in the theatre or even cinema – the recent movie version of *Polygraph* was largely filmed as a work-in-progress – this book thus became a truly collabo-rative effort, a literary game of tennis where we kept sending the ball back and forth. What one of us put into the process helped the other lead it further – and so the book became a blending of forces and personalities. In this sense, I believe that the nicest thing said in reviews of the French edition of this book was that it 'has two heads, but (practically) a single voice'.

All in all, only one convention of standard interview books remains here: the interviewer's words are written in italics, and the interviewee's words are in roman charac-ters. My task wasn't limited simply to asking questions and recording answers: italics are used as much for comments, notes and introductions as for setting up questions. The form of the text varies from chapter to chapter to suit the subject being discussed. There are a few segments of questions and answers which are transcribed directly as they happened, but other chapters were constructed as coherent essays by Lepage – often because a continuous exploration of a particular theme had quickly emerged in our discussion – while imaginary dialogues were assembled from disparate bits and pieces and yet other chapters were built up in more playful or analytical ways. I wrote introductions to chapters only when I felt they were necessary – sometimes Robert's words spoke for themselves and I did not see what I could add to them. This irregular form came quite naturally in the course of our 'tennis match', as did the general organisation of the sections.

As I was finishing the original French manuscript, I was already having a hard time telling which idea had come from whom. Throughout the process, a type of spontaneous convergence seemed to surround our work. Common references appeared at every step and coincidences kept popping up at each turn. For instance, events told in the chapter entitled 'Chaos' caused me to change the dates of my stay in Stockholm, in turn causing me to take a train to Copenhagen in order to catch a plane to London, a train which passes right by Elsinore castle. The next day, I was going to see an excellent production of . . . *Hamlet*, by the Peter Hall Company. And meanwhile, Robert and I had talked often of his forthcoming solo show: neither of us knew it at the time, but the show was to be called *Elsinore*. Coincidence followed coincidence. Later on, I was about to suggest that the immense sadness found in the music of the Bristol trip-hop band Portishead, which I had first listened to when working on our interviews, would fit nicely in his first movie, *The Confessional*, when Robert informed me that it had just been selected for its soundtrack.

On another night of transcribing our talks, I distractedly pulled a book by Stig Dagerman off my shelves; in it, I found a strong connection to a chapter of this book, 'Freedom and Slavery'. When I presented the book to Robert, he informed me that the acting coach on *A Dream Play* in Stockholm had been none other than the actress Anita Björk, who was the wife of Dagerman until his untimely death. Just before Robert had left Stockholm, she had given him a book: a collection of short stories by Stig Dagerman, as a token of the connections she saw between her husband and the director she had worked with throughout the autumn. Encouraged to read further, I was struck by Dagerman's writings on the theatre: Robert Lepage quipped one day that he could have written these himself. It was only partly a joke. These are only a few examples of the 'connecting flights' which infused this project even beyond the date of its first publication.

People who work with Lepage often say that the universe seems to speak to them as they are creating a play with him – that the themes and subjects evoked keep popping up everywhere they look. At times, everything seems to connect, just as the various aspects of Robert Lepage's work and life seem intimately linked.

For a good while, the working title of the book was *Pile et Face* – literally the two sides of a coin. It has seemed to me that these interviews constantly show both sides of a translucent medallion, two sides which are complementary rather than opposite. For Robert Lepage, process is the essence of a work's result, intimate life seeps onto the stage, organisation and logistics are inseparable from creation. Just as form is inseparable from content, different cultures and national identities constantly mesh together, while paradoxical links between chaos and creation or freedom and slavery seem quite fundamental.

This translucent quality in his work also shows up in the

formal aspects of Lepage's directing. Over the last year, I have been amazed to see how much Robert's work now shows its technical aspects, how the sleight of hand is presented in full view of the audience (I am thinking particularly of *Elsinore*) yet retains its magical properties, which is a sure sign that there is substance behind, or rather within, the formal inventions.

Robert Lepage has worked with everything, from the gigantic proportions of rock concerts to intimate shows where the most private of sentiments are shown with discretion and subtlety. Over the years, he has shown a remarkable ability to play with different art forms on different scales, respecting each genre's particular needs and rules. As I write this, after seeing the first stages of the 'final' version of *The Seven Streams of the River Ota*, I can only be impressed at the extent to which these various disciplines now seem to coalesce.

In our very first interview for this book, Robert Lepage said to me: 'I have the feeling that I'm heading somewhere different, doing different things, but I don't really know what they are yet.' With *Seven Streams*, this journey into the heart of theatre continues, and *Connecting Flights* provides many indications as to where it is heading. Where it will lead is still an open question, since Lepage and his collaborators always present us, as a friend of mine so aptly remarked, with the process itself, and not the final result of a process.

Over three years of almost constant work, *Seven Streams* has been turned on its head more than once. Between the fall of 1995 and the spring of 1996, just about every part of it changed yet again, leaving some critics dumbfounded. For the players in this team, however, it was not just a question of moving things around, but rather a way of letting the play speak its mind, of making its meaning and structure emerge freely. It's interesting to see, in fact, how much this show, even more than the previous ones, has incarnated Peter Brook's idea of theatre as a moving object, a thing which draws life from its own evolutionary process, and which begins dying once it becomes too settled.

Peter Brook was among the audience who saw the première of the full-length *Seven Streams* in Quebec City, and his reaction was more than enthusiastic. In an open letter to a Montreal daily newspaper, he wrote: 'Robert Lepage and his collaborators have given themselves a task that is as immense as it is deeply needed. They seek to create a theatre where the terrifying and incomprehensible reality of our time is inseparably linked to the insignificant details of our everyday lives – details that are so important to us, so trivial for others. For this, they are experimenting with a theatrical language where today's technology can both serve and sustain the humanity of a live performance. What a splendid task! What heroic ambition!' (Peter Brook, June 1996)

I can only hope that this book will indeed have shared in such an endeavour and remain a fitting record of a journey which I shared with Lepage but which for him continues.

Rémy Charest
Quebec City and Manitoulin Island, 1996.

MEMORIES

I write to you from my vantage point
beyond all territorial boundaries, in a
nocturnal sky that still boasts some
semblance of freedom . . . I shun
doctrine and no doubt you will see but
poorly what emerges from my words,
since I wish not to draw anything out of
them myself. Should something emerge,
it will do so of its own accord.

Jean Cocteau, translated from
Lettre aux Americains

To write, to create, you have to be a bit of a mythomaniac.
You have to be able to amplify the stories you hear, give a
larger dimension to the stories you invent. This is how you
transform them into legends and myths. So there's a very
close connection between mythology and mythomania, a
connection that has a lot to do with the world of story-
telling and memory.

Mythology is linked to the handing down of shared
stories from generation to generation. Problems of male
identity, according to men like Robert Bly, author of *Iron
John*, result from the loss of male myths. The loss of female
myths is much less obvious because mothers continue to

hand down values and traditions to their daughters. As men, we have Uncle Bob's fishing stories. Fathers also used to teach their trade to their sons, but this is mostly lost now. Women, at least, have maintained their maternal connection from one generation to the next.

Generally speaking, our society has lost its oral memory. Instead, we rely more and more on written or visual documents to immortalise the past, to store the things we remember, our history; and, as a result, our memory doesn't function any more because it no longer has to make the effort to store things. So, memory no longer distorts facts by filtering them, which makes it all the harder for history to be transformed into mythology.

Poetry and art depend on our ability to recount events through the imperfections of our memories. If we rely on records, written texts and photographs, we re-experience events essentially as they happened. This kind of truth is interesting to archivists and historians, but mythology has been largely eliminated from the process. It's not so important if a fishing story is true or not. What really counts is how we transform events through the distorting lens of memory. It's the blurred, invented aspects of story-telling that give it its beauty and its greatness.

In our own conversations, there are probably facts I could be more precise about, but I'm not interested in a documentary approach. Memory is much more important, much more essential. I remember telling a group of friends about an incident that took place in public at the opening of *Tectonic Plates* – or so I thought. It took Lorraine Côté, one of the principal actors in the show, a long time to convince me that in fact it had occurred during an evening rehearsal. This kind of misperception has helped me to see that our memories are often false, or close to being false.

In fact, Lorraine herself once told me a story in great detail, one she had told many times and that she saw clearly in her mind. But when she brought it up at a family dinner, everyone stared at her in surprise because she hadn't even been born at the time it had taken place. Yet she had remembered it with such precision. She had probably been told the story when very young and, through some obscure trick of memory, had given herself a role in it.

Our entire past is like that. We add and remove colours and people completely unconsciously. My mother invented a whole mythology that way. When I was young, she used to recreate the whole of the Second World War for me and my brother and sisters out of her CWAC (Canadian Women's Army Corps) notebooks and a few photos. She may have invented some things. Or her memory may have been imperfect, placing real events next to others that she had made up. What matters, however, is that through this process she was able to recreate the entire war. People complain about the unreliability of memory, but we should rejoice in it, use it as a creative tool.

Robert Lepage
Quebec City, 1995

GEOGRAPHY

TRAVEL LOG

Excerpt from a conversation held on 17 September 1994, at the Grand Hotel Restaurant, Stockholm, between 10 p.m. and midnight.

Can we begin to outline, right from the start, some of our goals, some of our reasons for having these conversations?

Maybe we should do it at the end. Doesn't a work's *raison d'être* appear more clearly after it's done?

Possibly, but don't you think it's also useful to give ourselves some guidelines?

Let me give you an example. Christopher Columbus's travel log reveals two things. First he was aware of the need to document, on a daily basis, a risky adventure whose outcome was still unclear. Second, he was aware that the adventure was bigger than he was; he suddenly found himself on a new continent and he had no idea what awaited him there.

Theatre is an adventure that's bigger than we are; an adventure which we embark on with many questions, but virtually no answers. I know the name of the continent we are planning to discover. But even after a few trips, not much else is clear. I came here to Stockholm to direct *A Dream Play* by Strindberg because an important Swedish theatre company invited me, but also because the invitation gave me the opportunity to explore and better understand my own way of working. Crossing geographic borders is also a way of crossing artistic borders, and perhaps it makes sense to keep a log throughout these journeys. At this point in my career, I think I have good intuition, and a sense of adventure that can inspire people, which allows me to say to actors, 'Drop the TV series. Let's go round the world.' But I don't have any answers.

I also have the feeling that I'm heading somewhere different, doing different things, but I don't really know what they are yet. At this point, I feel my work is beginning to intersect with the work of many of the artists with whom I have collaborated or artists with whom I intend to collaborate. *The Seven Streams of the River Ota* is a first attempt at working in this new way, at creating a meeting ground. Generally speaking, theatre belongs to the world of literature. Everything begins with a text. But I find myself more than ever returning to the idea of the theatre as a meeting place for architecture, music, dance, literature, acrobatics, play, and so on. In all my shows, this is what has interested me most of all: gathering artists together, combining different styles and disciplines. Cocteau and da Vinci were gatherers – of styles, of artists, of disciplines – and this is what has inspired me to talk about them.

Our production company Ex Machina, which is taking its first steps as we speak, is just beginning this journey of discovery, this gathering process. We still need to define, both collectively and individually in the company, who have been our major influences and which paths we are drawn to follow. The shows we have created are not written down, mostly because our work is perpetually changing, but also because things such as sound, images and the energy of play, are extremely difficult to describe. To fill this textual void, we have to tell what can be told and try to clarify what drives us.

We can begin to define our work through the three elements contained in the name Ex Machina. First of all, the word theatre has been dropped, since it's no longer our exclusive concern. With Théâtre Repère, which produced *The Dragons' Trilogy*, *Circulations* and *Tectonic Plates*, we created shows using the Repère method,[1] and we learned a lot from that way of proceeding. Second, the name Ex Machina evokes machinery. But for me, machinery is not only the harness that makes Cocteau fly in *Needles*, it's also inside the actor, in his ability to speak the text, to engage with the play; there are mechanisms in that, too. Third, we removed the 'Deus' from the expression, which originally heralded an unforeseen outcome, although I think we've preserved a mythical dimension and a sense of spiritual quest. The outcome and the narrative mechanism are still unforeseen, mysterious, and it's now up to us to uncover them. It's possible that, along the way, everything in our work will have been turned inside out, but this would be consistent with the company's name.

SET CHANGE

I've often talked about the story-telling talents of my mother and other women in the family. In fact, a large part of *The Dragons' Trilogy* deals with my mother and the women of her generation. It's an incredible sight to see all the women of the family gathered together and telling their stories. Their natural talent had a strong influence on me. But now that I think back, since my father's death in 1992 I have come to realise that he was a great story-teller in his own way, and that perhaps I learnt more from him than I first thought.

My father was a taxi driver. Until the seventies, taxis in Quebec often gave tours of the city and, because my father was perfectly bilingual, he was one of the drivers the good hotels recommended to their patrons. My sisters and brother and I were very impressed because sometimes people even sent us gifts to show their gratitude. Once, I remember, an American jeweller sent us all Swiss watches. Since we weren't particularly well-off, this was a big thing, and it made us very proud of our father.

A couple of times, he took me with him on his tours and I would listen to him tell the history of the neighbour-hoods, the city, the country. On the big tours, we went as far as the Montmorency Falls and then to Sainte-Anne-Beaupré Basilica. Before they built the autoroute, it took an hour to go and an hour to come back, so you really had to find something to keep the tourists busy. You had to have something to tell, and my father always came up with new stories. He would add details and fiddle around with the facts to make sure there was enough material. Exaggeration and embellishment are essential tools for both guide and story-teller.

If you think about it, the journey between Old Quebec and the Falls, and then between the Falls and St Anne's Basilica, is just like a very long scene change in the theatre. To fill the time, you have to embroider. My father would give facts – about the St Lawrence River, the sand bars, about the Île d'Orléans and the famous Québécois singer, Félix Leclerc, who lived there. But there were also long stretches of road where you really were stuck between two scenes. So he padded. I'll always remember the tiny house on the side of the road just outside Quebec City. My father would point to it and say, 'A family with eighteen children lives there.' The tourists would obviously be very impressed and surprised by the size of Québécois families; and then my father could go on with more factual information. His most beautiful stories were often told in the empty spaces.

It seems to me that a similar thing occurs with Shakespeare's soliloquies. The long monologues in *Hamlet* were probably used as a way of holding the audience's attention while the sets and props of the Elizabethan theatre were moved around in order to shift the scene from the ballroom of Elsinore Castle to its ramparts. I would guess that it was thanks to the scene changes that the most beautiful Elizabethan monologues were written. All great works make provision for transitions and sometimes what is done to fill the moment can become great art in itself.

In *The Dragons' Trilogy*, Lorraine Côté played both a nun and Stella, a mentally handicapped girl. Stella was being placed in an institution, and we had a scene in which the nun gives instructions to Stella's mother, which was immediately followed by another scene in which Stella was taken by her mother to the psychiatric hospital. There wasn't enough time for Lorraine to switch costumes, so I told her to wear Stella's costume under her nun's tunic and when she ran backstage she would only have to take off one set of clothing. But this still didn't work. So we had to have her take the tunic off in front of the whole audience. Jeanne, Stella's mother, undressed the nun, one piece at a time, and placed each piece of clothing in her daughter's suitcase, so that Lorraine was gradually transformed into Stella. To make it believable and to justify the transformation, we had to invent a whole story to go with it: the cornet became a symbol for the mind, the surplice a symbol for the heart, and so on. We invented a whole ritual to give the transformation meaning and it became one of the most beautiful moments of the entire six hours of the *Trilogy*. All because one actor didn't have the time to change costumes.

These mundane technical constraints force you to define your terms clearly, to justify what you're saying But if necessity is the mother of invention, doing it the other way round is much more difficult. In *The Seven Streams of the River Ota*, we came up with a scene in which each of the characters who has worn a particular kimono in the play appears in it by turn and then disappears, as if by magic. We knew that if we got it to work, the scene would be magnificent. But the idea didn't come out of a technical constraint All the accidents, all the constraints we experienced in preparing our shows inspired interesting ideas and scenes without too much difficulty. With this scene, which was not technically problematic, we had to work much harder for it to take shape and to find its place in the show.

Throughout the creative process, you're struggling and

searching, and, at a certain point, you open a door, invent a scene, a movement, an image. Sometimes it's beautiful, but then it remains on the surface, a pretty invention, nothing more. Sometimes, without realising it, you find something that touches the audience, and even something that might transform the audience. But one has no control over that. Picasso said that an artist's task is to discover things and then to find out what they are. That's absolutely true. There can be a huge gap between intention and result. Often poets will write up a rhyme, a pretty phrase, or a new expression, and only afterwards will they search for what's hidden behind it. We have to learn to accept that meaning comes to us after the fact.

I'VE NEVER BEEN TO CHINA

21 January 1995, Quebec

The character named Pierre Lamontagne, whose life resembles your own in certain ways, regularly appears in your work. At a press conference you gave when you started filming The Confessional, *you introduced him as 'an all-purpose character'. Where does he come from and what do you mean by 'all-purpose'?*

When you're young, sometimes people ask you what other names you might choose for yourself. I felt that I was more of a Pierre than a Robert. We often attribute meaning to a name and the meaning of Pierre [a stone] was very appealing to me. During an improvisation in *The Dragons' Trilogy*, I was working on a character who was about my age and, in some ways, my *alter ego* – an artist whose mother had been in CWAC, among other things. The decision to call him Pierre came quite naturally. His family name, which in itself is very meaningful [Lamontagne means 'the mountain'], actually came from earlier improvisations: Pierre's mother, played by Marie Gignac, was called Françise Roberge until she married a Lamontagne. So her son obviously became Pierre Lamontagne.

After this, the stone and mountain images took on huge proportions in the show. Pierre Lamontagne's name revealed both the littleness of the character and the vast scope of his ambitions. When, at the end of the *Trilogy*,

33

Pierre meets Yukali, the Japanese woman, in the art gallery, he discovers that her name means 'precious stone'. This is how a connection between the two is made and the scene becomes a meeting between West and East, Yin and Yang; the two characters are then compared to two stones in a Zen garden.

This meeting makes sense of all that has happened up to that point in the *Trilogy*, since what precedes Pierre's and Yukali's meeting is Stella's burial – the act of digging in the ground. By pointing out later on that a stone is the opposite of a hole in the ground, we were able to create an image of survival and continuity. Their meeting helps fill the void left by previous generations. In this way, the entire *Trilogy*, the entire history that precedes him, becomes Pierre Lamontagne's inheritance.

The movement in *The Confessional* is in the opposite direction: Pierre investigates his family's past by seeking to make sense of his father's death and his brother's disappearance. It's through Pierre that the truth will finally be revealed. In *The Seven Streams of the River Ota*, he finds himself in Japan and it's through him that the audience can make a connection with Japan and Japanese culture.[2]

So Pierre Lamontagne is a linking character, a vehicle. He's all-purpose because he is relatively young and an artist, which allows us to place him almost anywhere, in almost any circumstances. He's a very flexible, very mobile character – a blank character, in a way. He provides the link between the story and the audience. His naïve approach towards the events he encounters reflects the spectator's position. In the *Trilogy*, Pierre doesn't know anything about China. In *The Confessional*, he's not aware of his family's secrets or of those behind the filming of Alfred Hitchcock's *I Confess*. Through his curiosity and the discoveries he makes, such a character becomes a doorway or, better yet, a key for the audience, who therefore identify more easily with him and can use him to gain access to the play's core.

Over the course of his incarnations, the character developed a few inconsistencies. In *Seven Streams*, he came to Japan in 1995 to study calligraphy. At the beginning of *The Confessional*, he has just come back from China for his father's funeral, which takes place in 1989. However, to receive a methodical introduction to oriental culture he should have gone to Japan before China, since one learns most visiting in this order. Japanese culture draws most of its traditional origins from China.

You yourself have been to Japan, but have yet to visit China.

Yes, but I'm not really sure I'll ever go to China. My work, however, has preceded me there since our play *Polygraph* toured in Hong Kong. Moreover, Marie Brassard, who, of course, performed in *Trilogy* before working on *Polygraph*, told me when she got back how much of what we had imagined of China was true to life.

Both you and the other co-creators of The Dragons' Trilogy *have said that this show, which is so centred on China and the Orient, would never have seen the light of day had you actually visited China.*

For about ten years now I've been learning about Indonesian culture – its theatre, its music, its dance. For all intents and purposes, I'm an expert, but I've never set foot in Indonesia.

There is the physical place and then there's what the place represents for you. The China of the *Trilogy* was a China that suited what we wanted to say in the production. And the country itself is something like that, but it's also many other things. China has its smells, its textures, its rules, its sensations, none of which we know, but none of which we needed for the show. It's not important to be geographically precise. It's like our use of an anecdote:

what's important is that it fits in the show. Take Mother Courage's trials and tribulations in Europe during the Thirty Years War: if you map them out her movements appear disorderly, even impossible, but that's not what counts.

My fascination with the East also helps me to understand the West. For many years now, the former has helped me understand the latter. How can you understand the West, the culture of the twentieth century, when you're a Quebecer with virtually no cultural means at your disposal to interpret the world? You need a mirror, and one of my first mirrors was the East. In *Seven Streams*, mirrors are pervasive. They help to funnel Jana Čapek's memory, bringing her back to Theresienstadt, the Czech concentration camp. We also have the reverse, the complete absence of mirrors in the life of a *hibakusha* – a victim of the Hiroshima bomb – whose mother-in-law won't let her see her disfigured face. At one point in the show's development, there was even a game of mirrors between two of Marie Gignac's characters, twins whose lives have taken two completely opposite paths. When you look in the mirror, you see your opposite: a right-handed person sees a left-handed person and vice versa. It's like seeing the world turned inside out.

Geography is always present in your works. I seem to remember hearing you say that you thought of studying geography before you turned to theatre. It's even a line in Needles and Opium. *Is this true?*

Throughout my childhood, the artist in the family, in my eyes, was my older brother, Dave – not me. First he was an illustrator, then he became a photographer. Today he's a professor of photography at an architecture school in Ottawa. We shared the same room and so I could watch him as he worked, drawing and creating. I admired him enormously and I never thought I could do something similar.

I was interested in cartography because I did well in geography. In the tenth grade, I was top of my class in the subject. I talked a lot with my teacher and was genuinely interested in more than just population density and surface areas. Anyway, the more we learned about it, the less statistics played a role, and the more the subject revealed to us new ways of thinking. Without having read that much, I quickly found I had things to say about cultures, human geography, languages, travel, and so on.

Maps also offer us ways in which to give the world an intelligible form. This appears in our productions through our way of integrating different places and periods, of telling distinctive stories about these places. When you actually travel, you discover the essence of a country or a city, you perceive what makes it unique, what its soul is made of. In this sense, the shows are travel narratives and their success can perhaps in part be measured in the same way as we measure the success of a trip. We are either travellers or tourists. A successful production communicates a traveller's experience. To take up an image that the Montreal theatre critic Robert Lévesque used in his review of *Tectonic Plates*: a failed show, or at least a show that hasn't achieved a deep resonance, rather resembles a series of postcards brought home by a tourist who has seen ten cities in two weeks.

MIRRORS AND REFLECTIONS

Tuesday, 14 February 1995. The day after a public rehearsal of The Seven Streams of the River Ota *on the train from Quebec City to Montreal.*

Last night, I was struck by Jana Čapek's description of Pierre Lamontagne. She spoke of his 'lack of facial marks' and of the 'transparency' of his character. Seeing him in a way as your double, I thought I noticed certain similarities here with your own character, especially the flexibility and capacity for transformation that you yourself are known for. And Jana announces this just as she's about to make Pierre cross-dress as a woman, something you have also done in certain roles, notably in Tectonic Plates.

Yes, that's true. And there are other things she said earlier in the play and that remain just as true even though they have been eliminated from the dialogue. She showed Pierre photos of her friend Ada and said, 'I like this light because it brings out her masculine side. It's hard to find the woman in this woman.' Then, she took Pierre's face and said, 'You, on the other hand, are very feminine. It's very easy to find the woman in you.' And this is when she made him up and dressed him as a woman to show him just how easy it was. All of this explains how this character, a sixty-year-old lesbian who has never slept with a man, could then be attracted to Pierre and seduce him.

At this stage of our work, the gender references have been replaced by references to the pain hidden in Ada's face, which is why we ended up focusing on facial marks, the scars that people visibly bear, which really reflect their inner scars. It's mostly in this sense that she sees Pierre as having no marks. In fact, earlier in the play, Jana tells Ada that Pierre is as transparent as a piece of rice paper waiting for calligraphy. He's like a blank page, full of possibilities.

Physically, this is also an image that fits you.

I'm often told this by make-up artists in theatre, TV and film. They see my face as a blank page, which allows them to start from scratch. I don't have many facial marks, eyebrows, and so on.

In fact, it's often been said that your body is a real objet de théâtre, *which you can transform at will.*

For a while, this was one of the reasons I was in demand as an actor. But I never consciously linked these two things.

And when you incorporated it into Pierre Lamontagne's character . . . ?

It never occurred to me. Now that you mention it, I see it's true. But until this moment, I hadn't thought of it.

THE TRANSPARENT EMPIRE

The Meetings between East and West are frequent in Robert Lepage's work, as evidenced especially by The Dragons' Trilogy *(anchored as it is in the Chinatowns of Canada) and* The Seven Streams of the River Ota *(in which Hiroshima plays host to a series of Western characters, principally from Quebec). Japan in particular seems to draw Lepage, an attraction which was already evident in his first one-man show,* Vinci, *in which his tie bore the inscription 'kamikaze' in Japanese characters, in counterpoint to the Italian Renaissance that dominated the production.*

On his first visit to Japan to direct Macbeth *and* The Tempest *at the Tokyo Globe Theatre in 1993, Robert Lepage was struck by the country's very modern, very technological character. 'I feel as if I'm living in a Nintendo game,' he joked to Quebec journalists in a conference call from Tokyo. After several trips, however, he has now developed a deeper sense of the permanence, transparency and refinement of Japanese culture. He offers us a vision of a baroque culture that adapts the West to its own devices rather than imitating it; and a perception of Japan's discreet but extremely powerful influence on the culture of the West, which in turn remains seemingly unaware of the extent of Japan's influential presence – a presence far more extensive than that of cars and electronics.*

Where does your interest in Japan come from?

Just as children in the West often confuse Spanish and Italian cultures, so China and Japan are often confused. This confusion is not entirely unfounded, though, since the two cultures are related. Japan's cultural foundations are in China, and its principal language is of Chinese origin; the Japanese write with *kanji*, Chinese characters, from which they derive typically Japanese characters such as *katakana* and *hiragana*. The two countries have influenced each other and their histories have often intertwined through confrontation. As neighbouring states, Japan and China are deeply connected, much like the United States and English Canada. It is always a question of one cultural empire influencing another, and the way the influence manifests itself depends on the period.

My fascination with Japan began when I was sufficiently mature to be able to distinguish it from China and to perceive all the refinement of its culture. The insular culture of Japan seems to have brought about a kind of purification and transparency that the culture of mainland China never developed, or only in a small way. My point of view is that of someone who has a strong interest in geography. I believe the primary reason for the differences between these two cultures has to do with the nature of their territories, of their space. On my first visit to Japan, I was fascinated by the minuteness, by the maximised use of living space, and therefore by the forced transparency of everything in the country. Japan is a country made of rice paper – the walls of houses are literally made of it – so boundaries are always a little ethereal, hazy; they're made of air. There are countless demarcations, hierarchies, territories within territories, but they're all transparent.

In a couple of his books, Michel Tournier draws comparisons between Canada and Japan, between an immense land, almost devoid of population, and a land that is confined and extremely densely populated. This distinction, in my mind, has many consequences: The Japanese live in apartments the size of handkerchiefs, which means that they have had to create a considerable interior space, an infinite one. In Canada, space is available in a very concrete and obvious way; we have the potential to develop an interior space, but tend not to because of our conditioning, because of our perception of space.

I observed this during rehearsals when I worked with Japanese actors at the Tokyo Globe Theatre. Here in the West, during a break with actors, we tend to hang out, talk about this and that, catch up on news. But I noticed that doing this with Japanese actors seemed to violate something precious for them. All the actors have their own private spot in the rehearsal space to which they return during breaks. To approach them then is to invade their personal space. At first they are polite, but despite their politeness, you notice that you're robbing them of a private time during which they take refuge within themselves.

You can also see it in the actors' performances, which are ruled by an inner vocabulary. This is the whole basis of *buto* dance – initially inspired by *hibakusha* – which is about animating an inert, dead, body with a poetic spirit. Those who have mastered this discipline have learned to develop a series of inner images… waterfalls in their knees, floating clouds in their arms, and so on. The dancer creates an extremely compact universe. The richer and more colourful this universe, the bigger this poetic landscape, the better the movement. As a result, both in *buto* and in theatre, their passion is mostly an inner one. What you see on the outside is always infinitely subtle. You see the trace of an emotion, never the emotion itself. In the West, we have a tendency to reveal everything, to throw ourselves against walls as a way to indicate passion. The Japanese just show traces, not unlike their prints, their art of leaving traces on paper. They disclose only just enough to allow you to imagine an inner poetic landscape. This is much more powerful.

You also feel their need to retreat within themselves in their day-to-day lives. For example, the Tokyo Metro employs people to squeeze passengers into the cars with big sticks. The first time you experience this, you feel quite shocked, constricted and uncomfortable. But people there endure it with great patience. They don't shout and there's no panic. They understand the need for compression and so they just contract themselves. They don't explode as people would, for example, in the Paris Métro. It's almost as if they implode. I find this admirable. I think you have to visit Japan to understand their compressed sense of space, which permeates the whole culture, the theatre and even the landscaping of parks.

Doesn't this lack of space become oppressive?

You might think so, but it doesn't. You become aware instead of a very precise form of spatial organisation that goes hand in hand with a tight codification of all gestures, objects, clothes, and so on. The semiologist Roland Barthes describes the importance of such codes in his book *Empire of Signs*, which sums up quite well this whole side of Japan. In fact, what is most difficult for a Westerner landing in Japan is that he is overwhelmed by a wide variety of signs, salutations, introductions, gifts, and so on. The smallest thing has its meaning and place. Air Canada had to apologise for a publicity photo of a group of young women in kimonos that had been reversed – when a kimono is fastened the wrong way round it means the person is dead.

My point is that their spatial organisation has very precise rules and this organisation removes much of what is oppressive in their maximised use of space. You are also often confronted by empty spaces, in temples, Zen gardens, and theatres. These are planned empty spaces that don't exist in daily life. In a world in which everything is built up and occupied, an empty space, precisely because it's not built up, is in fact a full space. That's why the Japanese meditate in front of Zen gardens, little empty places that help them plunge into their inner space. And that's also the great pleasure of experiencing Noh theatre, where the stage is completely denuded, completely empty.

You speak of theatre, but we haven't said much about Japanese art. Many Western artists show their work in Japan, but there are few Japanese artists who come to Canada. As someone who works there regularly, why do you think Japanese art is so rarely exported?

Again, I think it's connected to the notion of transparency. which allows them to put lots of things in a huge pile and still to see it all clearly. The density of Japanese culture is so great they have no difficulty inserting other cultures into their own, like a sheet of paper slipped into a pile. Every Sunday, in a street near Yoyogi Park in Tokyo, a stage is set up for rock groups of all kinds to perform on. You see Elvises, Marilyn Monroes, Led Zeppelins, etc. But they filter the music in a very different way from us. Our Elvis impersonators do everything they can to reproduce the King, but they do it less well than he did. The Japanese Elvises, if only because of their physical appearance, can't be American Elvises. So they do Elvis Japanese-style, giving him a specifically Japanese character. They don't imitate the West. They seem to transcend it.

These games of superimposition create a kind of 'pizza' style of working. In contemporary theatre especially, the companies always have a very baroque side to them, which creates a strange effect. They have no problem performing the role of a samurai to the music of Brahms or mixing very disparate techniques in the same show. This obviously creates a whole set of problems when it comes to exporting the work. Of course, there's also the fact that the yen is too strong now, so that productions from places like the National Theatre of Bunraku in Osaka are too heavy and costly to tour. But it's mostly that the confusion caused by the baroque nature of their work is very difficult for international festivals and distributors who want to produce it.

When I directed *The Tempest* in Tokyo, I was told that this character would be played by a kabuki actor, that character by a Noh actor, and the other by a Western-style actor. The great director Ninagawa creates huge shows that, even within a seemingly single style, quote a multiplicity of other styles. In his *Tempest*, the actors performed in the style of an epic Hollywood film on a stage purely inspired by Noh theatre. The Japanese are obsessed with narrative and the ritual of narrative, but for them there is absolutely no problem in mixing actors who have different approaches or styles of delivery. In Western theatre, the success of a play is often seen to rely on how seamless the whole thing appears. For the Japanese the overall style and the individual performance don't have to match; richness is found in diversity, in the meeting and shock of styles. In this respect, the whole is very unrestrained and contains a multiplicity of codes, much like Japanese society. For a Western audience, it's difficult to be confronted with so many different codes. *Buto*, as it's performed by a troupe like Sankai Juku, goes over much better internationally, probably because the world of dance is more open to different vocabularies and accepts a greater degree of abstraction. But in the theatre world, we don't understand Japanese codes and so we find it difficult to understand their plays.

You've incorporated an increasing variety of media, and hence

codes, into your most recent plays. In The Seven Streams of the
River Ota, *you incorporate, among other things, video, song,
Chinese calligraphy, opera. Actors from different backgrounds
work side by side with an opera singer. Is this a sign of Japanese
influence?*

Very directly. I wouldn't do this at all – or at least not to
this extent – if I hadn't gone to Japan. It's a direction the
company and I are more and more interested in pursuing.
Our work brings us regularly to Japan. The Japanese audience is therefore very important to us, which makes our
trips all the more valuable. I think it also has to do with the
CNN global village in which we live, where we know
everything about everyone almost instantly. It's a world in
which we borrow more and more and in which we
develop more and more ties between cultures. We are
necessarily moving in the direction of more superimposition, more integration.

*Even though it's difficult to export, doesn't Japanese culture have
some influence on Western culture, a little like it does on your own
work?*

Yes, but we don't really admit it or recognise it. The
Japanese insinuate themselves into our culture, they don't
force themselves on us, unlike, say, the Americans.
Historically, Western culture has sought to impose itself,
especially through conversion to Christianity. But that
didn't work in Japan. When the Portuguese Jesuits became
too insistent, the Japanese expelled them and shut the door
on Westerners for two centuries. But without being forced
on us, Buddhism and Zen philosophy have become
extremely influential here. I have many friends who have
turned to Buddhism, who have incorporated Japanese
philosophies into their own lives, without really making a
big deal about it.

But beyond the spiritual realm, the Japanese are also transforming our lives, transmitting their values to us, through miniaturisation and transistors. They influence our daily habits without our even noticing it. We now think with computers, which forces us to use a cryptology that is very similar to the basic cryptology of Japanese language. The computer chip represents an attempt to fit the maximum amount of information possible in a tiny space, which is also what Japanese writing does. The Japanese way of organising thought, images and even society is very close to the technological methods we are adopting. But, this is a chicken and egg situation. Does Japanese thinking make a technological world possible or is it the emergence of a technological world that leads us towards a Japanese one?

THERE AND BACK AGAIN

Often when we seek out the unknown, we end up discovering what we already know. A francophone Quebecer who doesn't speak a word of Italian and gets lost in Venice will feel he has a lot in common with any English Canadian who comes along right then. We feel we have nothing in common with English Canada at first, but in a foreign context, we suddenly feel very Canadian. We discover things that we share. Travel, the discovery of another world, of another culture, help bring this about. When talking to Swedish actors here, I keep surprising myself with the words, 'Of course, we in America . . .' And yet, God knows, I usually feel millions of miles separate me from Americans. I would probably feel very European if I found myself right in the middle of the Prairies.

The obsession we have with discovering other cultures is usually intimately linked to the discovery of our own culture. Ask a Quebecer living in China to define Quebec and he will be happy to answer you. He's very well placed to do so, even better placed than a Quebecer who's never left home.

For me, it was impossible to come home to Quebec to found a company without having learned things abroad, without having accumulated a certain amount of baggage. People often think that studying for three years at the National Theatre School or the Conservatoire will automatically make you an actor or director. Students believe that once they have this qualification they'll officially be able to work, but it's not that simple. The schools are there to help you accumulate experience; those who have done the programme are ahead of others who haven't. But theatre is much vaster, much more demanding than that. My thirst to travel is not just a wanderlust, it's a desire to see theatre in Europe, in Asia, in Africa, to show what I do, to compare approaches, and so on.

The meetings and exchanges I have abroad enrich my work and the work of my company, work that remains profoundly Québécois. This is what has motivated me to return to the province of Quebec and more precisely to Quebec City, where I grew up and which inspires me much like the Plateau area in Montreal inspires the play-wright Michel Tremblay. It's from Quebec that I want to make contact with the rest of the world. The Quebec theatres we call national, like the Trident in Quebec City, the Théâtre du Nouveau Monde and the Compagnie Jean Duceppe in Montreal, even the French branch of the National Arts Centre in Ottawa, all have very little contact with what's going on abroad. These are institutions, but very local ones. It's by creating a small centre in Quebec City with links to Peter Gabriel's Real World company, the Dramaten in Stockholm, the Royal National Theatre in London, to the most interesting places in the theatre world, that I'm able to broaden my horizons. In Europe there is a kind of healthy balance that enables Peter Brook, who is British, to head the Bouffes du Nord theatre in the north of Paris and to book shows from all over, while the American Bob Wilson largely produces his shows in Germany. We don't have this in Quebec. We haven't reached that point yet. But we'll need to start inviting others to Quebec the way we are invited elsewhere. Our traditional reflex of cultural protectionism in Quebec has made us a little xenophobic. We need to overcome this.

It seems that the only way to interact with each other and be appreciated here in Quebec is by exclaiming how ingenious, how intelligent, we are. The problem is that our society doesn't have the historical baggage, the strength of identity that we need to be able to be self-critical. When, for example, Denys Arcand argues that, in his view, 'Quebec has no real greatness in any field,'[3] it's a hard thing to hear, but there's a kernel of truth in his words that we need to be able to face up to.When you say the same thing in France, it doesn't disturb people as much because France is big enough to take it. When Arcand and I meet, we talk a great deal about Québécois artists, about Québécois culture. We have similar criticisms, as well as profound differences on other points, given the generational disparity and how differently we relate to Quebec. But we can discuss all these things openly. There is health in criticism and self-criticism, which collectively in Quebec we have yet to find.

Quebec is reluctant to admit just how diverse it really is. Fernando Arrabal, who never rejected his Spanish roots, could still denounce the fascist regime under which he lived for so many years. Spain wasn't defined by fascism, just as nationalism and sovereignism don't define Quebec. These are current ideas in Quebec, but they don't define Quebec. It's difficult to make Quebecers see the faces of the province that aren't the face of the majority, to make clear to them the image the rest of the world has of us. Quebec defines itself in relation to English Canada, to the United States, to France, and, much more than we would like to admit, in relation to England. But beyond these countries, it's utter darkness. Quebec knows nothing, for example, about German culture, which is fundamental to any understanding of the twentieth century. I would know nothing about it myself had I not had the privilege of being invited to work in Munich, of seeing some of Schiller's plays in Austria, and so on.

We define our world in a limited way and we must be aware of this to be able to move on. Yet the nationalist wave is leading us in the other direction. We're usually won over to a cause by being told we're the best, the smartest. Yes, we should be told of our strengths, but we should also be told of our weaknesses and how to overcome them. It's because of this that the nationalist idea entices me more when I am abroad than when I'm here in Quebec, since the discourse isn't the same. Once, when I was in Paris, I heard former Quebec premier Jacques Parizeau give a speech in which he defined nationalism in terms of opening out on to the world, in terms of a modern Quebec ready to open itself up to the outside. And in Toronto, in a brilliant speech he gave to the Canadian Club, in impeccable English, he spoke of the maturity of modern states and again of openness. But at the same time, at home in Quebec, we were hearing people talk of language protection, of fields of jurisdiction, of very narrow things. All this remains a little unclear to me. When I hear people speak of internationalism, I say 'Let's go for it', but they only do it some of the time. I'm not lukewarm. I'm just confused.

There are a lot of nationalists who are aware of our potential strength as a francophone presence within an English continent. This strength depends on our opening ourselves up to the rest of the world. Another former premier, René Lévesque, travelled throughout the world and saw what was happening elsewhere, as did Jacques Parizeau – who speaks much better English than his former federalist political rival, Robert Bourassa. A few in the bunch have some perspective, but I don't think that the rank and file nationalists, the Bloc Québécois nationalists who refuse to speak English in the House of Commons, are very open to the rest of the world. Refusing to speak

English is refusing to speak the lingua franca, a language that provides the link between the Japanese and the Swedish, between Germans and Latin Americans. I know that the invasion of English culture in Quebec provokes people, but we have to rise above such a limited perspective.

Right after she became editor of the Montreal newspaper *Le Devoir*, I met Lise Bissonnette on a plane to New York, where I was going to do *Polygraph* in a version that was two-thirds English and one-third French. She was going to give a lecture on Québécois culture. I asked her what language she was going to lecture in and she replied that it would be in English. So the question is, quite simply, what does more to promote the French character of Québécois culture? An English lecture or a show that's one-third French?

I don't think people really understand how important an achievement it was for us to perform *The Dragons' Trilogy*, two-thirds of which we did in French, for a month to packed houses in London. It was an important event. There were no subtitles, no simultaneous translations, and people still remember it. It even became a reference point in the theatre world. Don't you think that that kind of show has an important impact on people's understanding of Quebec? Yet, when someone puts English into a French show in Quebec, it's interpreted as being federalist or pro-Canadian. That's plain stupid.

I find myself emotionally very torn about nationalism as it's understood here. On the one hand, I believe in it in the sense that I think we're different and so we should assert and develop our culture. On the other hand, nationalism leads some people to become closed and exclusive, which I find extremely repulsive.

What effect do these attitudes have on relations between Québécois artists and the rest of the world?

What comes to mind immediately is that, in Quebec, people don't really understand one of the main facts about theatre. There are many actors who don't want to tour the way we do, who aren't ready to work at our pace. Even to get actors to come to Ottawa, when I was artistic director of French theatre at the National Arts Centre, was sometimes difficult. They would say they had kids at home, that Ottawa was too far, not interesting enough, and so on.

The actors who become involved in projects like the Shakespeare Cycle or *The Seven Streams of the River Ota* have made themselves available and are daring enough to commit to a difficult job, to tackle roles that are beyond them. Jacques-Henri Gagnon, who was my first Prospero in the Shakespeare Cycle, committed himself to doing what was extremely demanding work for him. He was prepared to do scene changes, to find himself in the wings on his knees, to take on an extremely rigorous touring schedule, and so on. He did an excellent job and, when he did leave, it was because the demands made on him were finally beyond his physical abilities. Jacques Languirand, who took over from Jacques-Henri, also agreed to tackle these kinds of challenges, learning a ton of lines in very little time, working in difficult conditions, especially for a man of his age. Marc Labrèche, who has taken over from me in *Needles and Opium*, knows he has to make sacrifices, to turn down offers of work so that he can take the play on tour. But people like this who are ready to take up a challenge are more the exception than the rule.

Conversely, it also happens that some actors leave us after only a brief stint because they prefer to work at home in Montreal. I can't work with people who won't make a long-term commitment. Actors often say they're afraid of being forgotten in their own city. They say they're afraid they won't be cast any more or that they have television parts waiting for them. Let them tour the world with us and see if they make a career for themselves. In my opinion, the problem is that Québécois artists are rarely interested in international travel. They don't see the usefulness of going to Germany or Japan.

I think that in Quebec the theatre lacks the kind of prestige that encourages people to make sacrifices, that makes playing in other cities or countries seem valuable. This prestige can exist anywhere. Under Jean-Marie Lemieux, the Théâtre du Bois de Coulonge in Quebec City – a summer theatre – had the kind of prestige that made actors want to leave other cities to perform there. But this kind of thing seems to have disappeared somewhat. In defence of Québécois actors, of course, they need to pay their bills like everyone else. A television series or an established theatre like the Compagnie Jean Duceppe in Montreal pays so much more than touring or working in little companies, and often the decision comes down to a simple question of money. If theatre paid better, the problem would partly correct itself.

Having said this, I still believe that, fundamentally, there is a pettiness we have to fight against in Quebec. I fight against the pettiness of my parents' world and the pettiness of the country and city I've chosen to live in. The image of Quebec that nationalists want to sell us is a petty one, even though they try to sell it as a big thing. I believe in it, but we have to realise that it represents something very small on a global scale. We have to make a point of informing Quebecers about what's going on elsewhere, of showing them what the world as a whole has to offer. We can complain about the pettiness, but we also have to act to counter it.

Homeward bound

22 September 1994. Bern's Restaurant, Stockholm.

Quebecers as a people define themselves by what they are not. We define ourselves negatively, as we see in current expressions such as *c'est pas pire* ('could be worse'); *ça va pas mal* ('I'm not doing too badly'); *c'est pas mauvais* ('it's not bad'). The media in Quebec also work that way. At one point, all the interviews I gave revolved around the same questions: 'People say about you that . . .' 'Don't you have a problem with . . .?' 'If you do this, isn't it because . . .?' Even in your own approach for this book the questions you ask follow this pattern. Several of your questions refer to what people perceive as missing in my work, to the difficulties that I come up against.

But doesn't this book offer you an opportunity to dot your 'i's and make clear exactly what it is you do think?

That's what you think. We eventually engage with the heart of the matter, but we often begin with a negative approach. We often touch on the hype, on what is false; that's all I hear discussed in Quebec. When I go to Germany, for instance, they interview me about my work. They talk about the impact it has. They ask me about my projects, not what I thought about such and such a critique. That kind of negative approach is typically Québécois. And I include myself in this criticism.

Yes. Your approach is to answer with 'elsewhere, it's not like this.'

People talk about the difficulties I have, about what is poorly understood in my work, but they hardly talk about my work. As a general rule, this is how my work is known in Quebec. This is because we are so profoundly obsessed with the lives of stars: that's what culture is to us. We like to identify ourselves with stars who have lived through some sort of traumatic event. People rarely stand out from the crowd and, when they do, they are a constant focus of attention.

When I performed *Needles and Opium* in Montreal three years ago, we played at the Nouvelle Compagnie Théâtrale because it was the only place that accepted our terms – that there be absolutely no promotion. This spawned considerable media coverage without my having to utter a single word to a journalist; it all just happened around me. It was at about that time that I was interviewed by Denise Bombardier for her show on CBC TV, *Raison-Passion*. I had promised to do this during an earlier interview but held off for a long time because I was afraid of being put in a box and having to spend a whole hour on television talking about my faults and difficulties. But she assured me that – unlike what she does with politicians – she didn't corner artists. Once this was settled, we did an extraordinary interview, one people still refer to. It was very sane. But you can't take this for granted.

But Quebec still remains the place where your work is best known . . .

No. I'm better known outside Quebec now. Statistically, London is where my shows have been seen the most. I don't mean just in terms of ticket sales – but also in terms of their impact.

Nevertheless, you have a longer-standing connection with Quebec.

Yes, and my relationship with my home country is certainly shaped by that. But I believe, however, that this also has to do with the way in which theatre is considered in Quebec, and what it represents culturally. And perhaps my work doesn't have that much of an impact on Quebecers now. I know that my work abroad hardly interests them. Maybe it has a greater impact on people in other countries. But I'm not sure I can do anything about that. And, if it's true, is it really such a big deal?

GLOSSARY

The differences in theatre vocabulary between one language and another reveal just how varied cultural logic can be. The immense, almost empty, stages of Japanese theatre explain a lot about Japan, the Japanese imagination and the ceremonial importance of space in their culture.

When I work in other countries, I always try to adapt, to adjust myself to these realities. That's the principal challenge of working internationally: to be able to compare methods, compare visions of the world, and – however gently or harshly we approach it – to find a common path that will lead us where we want to go.

Acteur, Schauspieler, Player

It's important to distinguish clearly between actors and players. In French, we tend to speak of *acteurs* in film and *comédiens* on the stage. In English and in Germanic languages, there is the notion of a game in the words 'player' and *Schauspieler* – literally, one who shows his playing – although, personally, I find that we see 'acting' on stage more often than 'playing'. The notion also applies to the idea of the theatrical work itself, the play. Although generally called *ein Stück* in German [literally, a piece], there is a German play based on *The Tempest* that's called *Sturmspiel*, the storm play; and *A Dream Play* in its original Swedish title is *Ett Drömspel*, which means both the dream play and the dream game. So, an underlying notion of playing prevails, in both its connotations of sports and a game. We play cards and hockey, we wonder *combien il y a de joueurs* – how many players? This also works for 'a play' in the theatre. The aspect of the game is less obvious in French when we speak of *acteurs*, of *comédiens*, of *une pièce de théâtre*. We do speak in French of an actor's playing *le jeu d'un acteur*, but the notion of a game is less marked.

These linguistic differences don't necessarily reflect a current reality, though. German actors are not necessarily more focused on playing just because the notion is inscribed in the German word for actor, *Schauspieler*. But you can perceive that there is something very significant in this way of naming things. For me, it's very important to restore the notion of playing to the game of theatre, by introducing competitiveness, games and sports. And with a transcendent aim: we watch beings made of flesh and bone enter the stage and, through play, become archangels and gods. In the same way, when we watch dancers, we admire their training. Their expanded superhuman bodies illustrate just what they represent; their bodies are theatrical objects representing the very notion of transcendence. Because it is muscled and defined, the body is amplified in the same sense that make-up amplifies the actor's face. It's through this physical reality that we have access to all the great themes and that we can bring out their essence.

In *The Dragons' Trilogy*, we see a nun, played by Lorraine Côté, who merges the ideas of Mao with Christian precepts and is swept away in her exaltation. Her words fly, and to create the impression of flight in physical terms, she balances herself in a tenuous position on a bicycle. Suddenly we're at the circus, but rather than cancel out the flight of her lyricism, this circus impression reinforces her words. These were ideas that came freely, without much profound reflection, but which enabled a kind of transfiguration through playing. One human being flies away, another transcends death, and ultimately we are able to discover much more about humanity than about divinity.

Audience and *Spectateurs*

Again, we're not talking about the same thing when we refer to the audience and to *les spectateurs*. While French-speakers and Italians come to watch a show, the British and, by extension all English-speakers, focus primarily on the word, on voice and on sound in the theatre. English audiences really come to hear us. They see language as sacred, they find the language hidden within the language. Maybe this is why writing and playwriting in English Canada are so strong. Quebecers' strengths tend rather to lie in directing, inventing, image-making. Some English Canadians have these particular strengths too, but they are most obvious among Québécois artists. This reveals a very significant division within Canadian culture. I don't say this to repeat a cliché, but rather to highlight the foundations of these cultures and their different ways of relating to the world.

Director, *Metteur en scène, Regissör*

The same notions can be applied to the idea of authority. In countries ruled by authoritarian regimes or monarchies, you will most often hear the Scandinavian word *Regissör* or Germanic *Regisseur*, with the sense of regimenting, ruling and legislating. It doesn't have the same resonance as *metteur en scène* [literally, one who puts things on the stage] which gives the impression more of an employee than a director. This is also true of the difference between a stage manager in English theatre and a *régisseur* in French theatre. Their roles are different, and so is the level of authority they exercise and the artistic contribution they make.

In German theatre, the director holds a great deal of responsibility because his leadership must be absolute. It's almost totalitarian, something we almost never see here in Quebec. If you don't direct that way, you won't be able to work there. A German actor I worked with explained that this doesn't reflect a fascist trait, but the opposite. According to him, after being told one too many times what to do by their leader, they decided that it would never happen again in the political realm, so they sublimated their need for leadership into theatre, teaching, and so on. German politicians today are good bureaucrats rather than great leaders. But in theatre, film, opera, what rules is the attitude 'tell me what to do',' 'push me'.

This kind of authoritarianism is completely antithetical to my way of working. When I was in Munich, I never wanted to take on that role. But on the very first day of rehearsal, everyone stood around waiting to be told what to do. Soon after the rehearsals began, I went to the assistant director of the theatre and said, 'They want me to yell at them.' I didn't think it was right to start out by yelling things at the actors, so the assistant director did it for me. What seems to be behind this authoritarian dynamic is a desire to be transformed, to be given the means to improve. Sometimes, we need our parents' authority to discipline us and orient us a little. German actors are essentially saying, 'Insult me if you have to, but direct me.' It's really challenging.

Perhaps there's a connection between the fact that Québécois theatre productions are more democratically run and that, conversely, we like strong political leaders, or, at least, we like them to be father figures. Just think of our relationship with Pierre-Elliott Trudeau: everyone in Quebec supposedly hated him, but we also followed him.

Having said this, the Germans produce extraordinary theatre. They have a system that works well, only I didn't function well in it. It was so bad that when my assistant, Philippe Soldevila, who co-ordinates most of my bookings, saw how much difficulty I was having, he all but called the Globe in Tokyo to cancel the directing job I had scheduled there a few months later. He was afraid that in yet another highly organised, very authoritarian country, I would experience the same problems. He told me, 'You're too soft to assert yourself or to make sure the same thing doesn't happen again.' He was also worried about how thinly I had spread myself over the past two years, with my constant travelling, and how little I had been able to create as a result. But I had a hunch that it would be different in Japan and, in the end, things went more smoothly there.

It's easy to find yourself skinned alive in a place like Germany. As a director, as a creator, you're constantly reminded of all your deficiencies, constantly having to face up to them. All of your talents are called upon, and if you have a weakness, one you have managed to hide throughout all your years of work, it'll suddenly be exposed. In Japan, by contrast, people are extremely respectful of your way of working, very deferential, and many things that would never have made it through in Munich did in Japan.

The best approach is probably somewhere between these two extremes. That's why things worked so smoothly in Stockholm. There were moments of difficulty, as in Germany, but people there were also extremely respectful. It was the best of both worlds, and I think it resulted in a good production, a surprising one, which took flight when all the pieces finally fell into place in the last few days.

Macchinista, Scénographe, Décorateur, Set designer

There's an important difference between the concepts of *scénographe*, *décorateur* and set designer. The duties of a designer involve the idea of invention and architecture much more than do the duties of a *décorateur*, whose concern is with ornaments and sets. The idea of spatial organisation is also very present in the word *scénographe*. In Italy, they prefer the term *macchinista*. The Italians are very well-known for their theatrical machinery: La Scala's is the most beautiful in the world. It looks like an enormous ship with sails, rigging and pulleys. It's a complex piece of engineering, with its traps and mechanisms, and this notion is reflected in the way the stage is used.

Thought (思)

For Westerners, thinking only involves the head. But in Japan, the heart is the driving force for thought. The ideogram for the word 'thought' displays a field (田) over a heart (心). The heart nourishes and helps ideas grow in the field. This image is very close to what for years I've called the intelligence of the heart.

When I work with actors, I tell them they have to play with emotion and intelligence. The combination of the two creates intuition, which is the intelligence of the heart. In Western culture, we tend to separate these two halves of thinking. We consider the emotional and the rational as two distinct entities. Among Japanese actors, on the other hand, the union of the two doesn't need to be explained. It's obvious in their way of working, and obvious, of course, in the fact that their word for heart is inscribed in their word for thought.

Shadow and Light

When we were working in Japan, Marie Brassard recog-
nised one of the employees at the Tokyo Globe Theatre
and she asked him if he was an actor. He was a technician
and he told her that he worked on the shadow side of the
production. He wasn't just using a poetic image. In Japan,
you either work on the shadow side or the light side, on
the side of reality or on the side of dreams. This says a lot
about their view of theatre, and about the role of the technician. Japanese Taoist consciousness is aware not only of
the light side of theatre, but also the shadow side. In other
words, they're aware of theatre as a whole, and what goes
on in the flies, the wings, in the control room, and at an
organisational level is just as important as what takes place
on stage. They reflect two aspects of the very same thing.

In Western theatre, things are divided in a different way,
since we speak of the *côté cour* and *côté jardin* in French, and
of stage right and stage left in English. In the first case, a
kind of poetic opposition is suggested: on one side is the
court, civilisation, order; on the other is the garden,
nature, escape. But, more prosaically, the idea relies on
principles of entrance and exit, which are true to all
theatre, but have tended to lose the depth of their original
meaning. The English case is curious since the designation
is contrary to what the audience sees. We see a world
turned inside out, where right and left are inverted, and
this brings us back to the notion of a mirror, of theatre as
a mirror of existence.

APPENDIX: I, WE, YOU

*Over the course of our conversations, Robert Lepage's choice of
words was intriguingly revealing. When speaking of his works,
even of his one-man shows in which he often presented very personal material, he tended to describe the creative process in the first
personal plural, using the pronoun 'we', or else the colloquial all-
inclusive 'you', thus putting a strong emphasis on the collective
aspect of his creative work. On the other hand, his use of 'I' when
describing his work at the Globe in Tokyo or the Dramaten in
Stockholm reveals the singular and sometimes solitary tribulations
of working abroad. His encounter with other ways of thinking or
acting was similar to that of a private individual experiencing a
foreign culture. The 'we' was exteriorised and became the other.*

*Generally speaking, this very singular creator seems to prefer
the collective refuge of the first person plural, which counters the
exclusive focus he receives from the public. In conversation, he uses
'we' as frequently, if not more frequently, than 'I'. The only
exceptions to this are moments when Lepage speaks about his
family, as you might expect, and when he reflects on the chaos of
his existence, which he acknowledges to be entirely his own.*

MYTHOLOGY

WHEN GENIUS COMES CALLING

Jean Cocteau wanted to popularise the
word 'genius' – so improperly deified by
the romantics – so that one could speak
like Stendhal of the 'genius' with which
such and such a duchess knew how to
step out of her barouche.
    Conversely . . .

Michel Tournier, translated from *Des
clefs et des serrures*

*When you compliment Robert Lepage or praise any of his various
talents as actor or director, he will more often than not be embar-
rassed by the comment and discreetly try to change the subject. For
example, when, during a conversation we had in Stockholm on 23
September 1994, I commented on his undeniable stage presence,
he entered into a long discussion on the physical nature of his
training at the Conservatoire du Québec, with hardly any reference to a more personal side of the issue. Without denying the
considerable pride he feels in seeing his work applauded and appreciated, it can be said without a doubt that he does not let himself
be swept away by the torrent of praise that follows him throughout the world.*

*That anyone might on occasion use the term 'genius' to describe
him, makes Lepage especially uneasy. The elusive nature of what*

goes into creating a genius has something to do with this, of course. In his work on the lives of several outstanding figures, among them Picasso, Stravinsky and Einstein, the American psychologist Howard Gardner carefully avoids the term altogether, preferring instead the expression 'creative individual'.[4] Robert Lepage would certainly approve, given his vigorous opposition even to the idea of 'specific genius', an idea close to Cocteau's notion of genius referred to above, which conveniently appeared in a conversation we had about the apparent ability of the director and his collaborators to make a show spring out of almost nothing.

21 September 1994. Restaurant of the Diplomat Hotel, Stockholm.

Eliciting meaning from a text or from the world that surrounds us is not easy. Some things exist in the world but are only noticeable when someone names them or gives them a meaning. Does Robert Lepage's specific genius reside in his ability to extract meaning from things?

Robert Lepage has no special genius. Genius is something different. It's a gift that doesn't really belong in our profession at all. My profession is simply what I do. Albert Einstein, for example . . .

Wasn't Einstein also doing his job, in other words resolving mathematical and physical problems? He asked new questions and discovered previously unknown equations. Isn't this what you do in the theatre?

Not really. We speak of genius when, for example, someone solves a huge mathematical problem overnight in a dream. But that's not how things work for me. My most interesting creations tend to have ridiculous beginnings. They have to do with things that are supposedly unworthy of theatre. It's easy to say – as common belief or aesthetic taste would have it – that your exceptional brain worked through a problem overnight and came up with all these answers, but it's just not true. The answers are found in the plays, in the work you do. They're not in your head. You're not the one who has them.

The discussion then shifted abruptly (largely through the fault of the interviewer) to why the term genius is so frequently used to describe the creator of The Dragons' Trilogy. *Lepage wondered how one could take seriously critics and columnists who 'cry genius one day and, soon after, consider you an idiot'? Then we got lost in an exchange on the tendency of artists to doubt themselves. Reviewing the transcript of our conversations the following May gave us the chance to develop further the ideas that were beginning to take shape above. And so we reached a definition of genius as something which lies outside the artist, an occurrence rather than a state of being – a definition quite similar to the 'creative break-throughs' that Howard Gardner sees as the necessary milestones in the career of an artist or thinker.*

Ultimately, genius has to do with convergence. In Robert Lévesque's critique of Montreal director Gilles Maheu's *Le Dortoir*, for instance, he wrote that Maheu had had the privilege of being visited by genius. We are the tools of genius. If it graces our lives it's because, in a sense, our radio is tuned to the right frequency. You have to have a certain amount of talent, a certain amount of intelligence and intuition to be able to call on genius. But genius isn't something that's inherent in our make-up.

And this is why you say that Robert Lepage has no special genius?

If people had only to rub me three times to make the genie appear, I could solve quite a few problems. If it was part of our make-up, all the work of those artists we call geniuses would be uniformly good. But being visited by genius has a lot to do with chance – and it might only happen once in a lifetime. What's necessary is to work constantly to invite it back. It might seem like a poetic image, a way to avoid talking in other terms about the issue, but this view seems very real to me these days.

It's a question of openness. To be graced by genius, you have to be receptive, to have your ears open. We all come to a production with preconceived ideas, but you have to be prepared to set them aside, smother your pride and always place the work first. Sometimes, it seems that a work could've been a masterpiece if the director or the author hadn't been quite so proud, if he had allowed the art to triumph. On occasion, during rehearsals for *Seven Streams*, I would stubbornly hold on to certain ideas for a particular scene. But you have to be prepared to let them go when other suggestions, other approaches, are obviously better. For personal reasons, of fame or reputation, we might want our initial idea to win out rather than give in to what comes up. But if you always have to prove that you're right, you'll make yourself miserable. And so I live more easily these days with mistakes and failure. Because mistakes are necessary.

This ability to admit to your mistakes, to give up on earlier convictions, inevitably involves doubt, a primordial condition of creation. People may think you have to find the answer, but what you need is to create the question. This struck me when I met great artists such as Ingmar Bergman, Peter Brook or Peter Gabriel. My first meetings with them weren't anything like gaining an audience with a great patriarch. From a distance, we see famous people as divine beings. But, in fact, their strength is in the very humanity of the questions they ask. These are people who seriously doubt themselves and the work they do. In his song, 'Only Us', Peter Gabriel sings, 'The further on I go, oh, the less I know', a claim some might find astonishing from an artist who has accomplished as much and knows as much as he does. Few people in theatre know as much about this artform as Peter Brook, but he seems convinced that he knows nothing about it. Despite all that he's accomplished, despite all his abilities, he can still find himself completely lost. In Woody Allen's film *Bullets Over Broadway*, the character of the playwright opens the film with the line, 'I'm an artist!' But at the very end, he says instead, 'I'm not an artist.' That's Allen speaking behind the character, and that's probably what he believes today. Personally, I haven't yet reached that level of doubt.

OPIUM

One of the most striking images of Robert Lepage's work is the screen projection of a huge syringe plunging into Miles Davis's silhouetted arm in his solo show Needles and Opium. *Though it may not always have been as directly illustrated, the theme of drug use and its various effects on the user have been present in almost all of the director's plays, in one form or another. For the director, the theme is important for its metaphorical qualities and because it allows for the transformation of perception, in characters as well as in audiences.*

I think that *Needles and Opium* marks a kind of culminating point in our use of the drug theme, which appears quite frequently in our works. In *Circulations*, there's a scene in which two guys and a girl are smoking a joint in a motel, quietly talking in the moonlight that's streaming in through a skylight above them. Then the stage goes to black and when the lights come up we see the same scene but through the skylight, in other words, from the point of view of the moon. It was the first time we used an inverted perspective in our work. The actors were stretched out horizontally, giving the audience the impression they were watching the characters from the sky, from above. And it was the use of drugs that made this kind of poetic transposition possible.

In general, although the drug theme is partly linked to the period and place in which the narratives unfold, it also provides a means for us to express certain metaphors. Drugs allow you to present things from a very different point of view on the pretext that a character is under their influence. So we can move from the level of realistic performance to one of poetry, showing different facets of a scene, depending on what the subject allows.

Drugs provide a transformative tool at both a scenic and narrative level. *Needles and Opium* revolves to a great extent around two artists, Miles Davis and Jean Cocteau, who both sought inspiration through drugs. But really they found inspiration the moment they stopped taking drugs. Miles made his mark only after his four years of intoxication and four weeks of detoxification were over. The same for Cocteau – also four years and four weeks. Cocteau found a certain kind of inspiration in opium, but it was mostly a balm for the pain caused by the death of his lover, Raymond Radiguet. And the pain of his detoxification brought about a genuine return to inspiration. The transformation doesn't only come about because the narcotics make you see cockroaches or alter your mood, but because they transport you to another level.

One of the most interesting things in *The Dragons' Trilogy* for me is the transformation of the British character, Crawford, whose journey from youth to death we witness. The evolution is even condensed in one of the scenes into a few seconds, when his coat is worn successively by the three actors who incarnate him at his three different ages. The first incarnation is the most naïve, most talkative, most funny of the three. Once he's introduced to opium by the old Chinese man, he enters a phase of greater maturity and he starts to turn inwards, and then as he ages he becomes totally mysterious. In the Second Dragon, he's already a little gone. In the train scene, where he meets Françoise, he has become a withdrawn, quiet character, when he had been very talkative in the first part. He asks her if she has ever smoked hashish. He's now become a drug dealer. This is a good example of a tool of character transformation.

Beyond its transformative effects, there's another constant in the drug theme in my shows, which is opium itself. In *The Dragons' Trilogy*, the opium that the old Chinese man introduces to Crawford leads us into a dance to the deadened beat of the drug. Heroin, a derivative of opium, plays a more or less central role in *Tectonic Plates*, in *Needles* and in *Seven Streams*. If I keep coming back to these drugs, it's because of' an experience I had when I was a teenager that left me in a state of depression for almost two years.

When I was fourteen, I tried drugs for the first time with a girl I was falling in love with. No big deal. We smoked tea and then a little marijuana, which didn't have that much of an effect on us. But one day, she had a fling with another guy. I was deeply affected, deeply hurt by the whole thing. I was discovering what it meant to be in love, which also meant accepting love's painful consequences. When I continued to do drugs in the following weeks, it had a different effect, and I had a really bad trip from a joint spiked with opium. For two years, I was prescribed antidepressants. I would go to school but would run straight home afterwards and watch TV. That's all I did.

I felt the state I was in was the result of the drugs, which I also connected to the notion of interchangeability, to the ambiguity of emotions and sexuality – in *Circulations*, the moon scene is followed by a love scene *à trois*. It took me a very long time to realise that my depression wasn't due to my bad trip, but even so, after those six months of experimenting, I rarely shared a joint at parties. I never really touched the stuff again. I'm now grateful to that bad trip for helping me to see the relative sides of reality and unreality and for pushing me to become introspective, which I wasn't inclined to be before.

To benefit from the experience, though, I still had to surface from my depression, and this I owe to my sister, Lynda, who pushed me really hard to act in my first play, *Le p'tit bonheur* by Félix Leclerc. It was often put on in drama classes at my high school, along with his *L'auberge des morts subites* because there were lots of parts for everyone. I liked the drama classes a lot, which I sort of had to take because the programme of studies required us to take one arts course a year and drama was just about the only option I hadn't taken.

But in the state I was in, I just couldn't imagine going on stage. First of all, I never went out of the house at night, and I couldn't see myself performing to a hall filled with people. But the group I was working with on the play were really counting on me because it had been going well and, while some of the others were scared and had given up their parts, I had kept up with all of my small parts. And I have to say I really liked the rehearsals. So my sister decided that enough was enough and that I would do the play. She would dress me up and put me in a taxi and I would cry. I didn't want to go. But she forced me to and in the end I did it, and it was a great success. And then I began to crave this appreciation which had liberated me from my state of withdrawal. It helped to bring me back out into the world.

By overcoming stage fright, I began to understand what it meant to conquer something – since stage fright gives you a terrible and inexpressible vertigo, but also an incredible adrenalin rush. Because overcoming stage fright had changed my life, I wanted to create a context in which I could throw myself into the battle every night and come out on top. So I made it my profession. Sometimes, it becomes almost more important than the play.

FROM THE GYMNASIUM TO
MOUNT OLYMPUS

Here, the word is entirely one with the
flesh. Each body is a mute and unwritten
poem.

Michel Tournier, in *Des clefs et des
serrures*, referring to the
tattooed, scarified and painted bodies of
Nuba warriors,
photographed in the Sudan by Leni
Riefenstahl.

Robert Lepage's creations are filled with recurring motifs, including a great variety of themes and rituals, objects and actions. In addition to his use of drugs, and particularly opium, we regularly encounter suicide, train trips, shaving, the moon and nudity. Very frequent in his works, nudity is only rarely linked to eroticism or revealed in the sexual act. It expresses, rather, an aesthetic reflection, an accentuation of the essence of a character and, of course, offers another means of framing an actor's performance and physical presence.

In my mind, the theatre is precisely where nudity belongs. In my shows, erotic tension tends to arise when people are fully clothed. Nudity, on the other hand, appears without this tension and reveals the fragility or the essence of a character. It's more a return to classical elements. The Greek gods and heroes weren't clothed. The word 'gymnasium' comes from the root *gymnos*, which means 'naked', and so it's the place where people are naked. In *Needles and Opium*, we use one of Erik Satie's *Gymnopédies*. The word, I was told, means 'bare feet', which is literally the case of the character on stage, even though it came about by pure mechanical necessity, because I had to take my shoes off to balance my weight in the harness I was suspended in.

Nudity is the presence of things in their pure state. When the actor is nude, he is free of his social envelope, of what socially defines the envelope of his body. When we see the lawyer naked in Strindberg's *A Dream Play*, we see him freed from the envelope that defines him as a lawyer. In a sauna, where everyone is naked or wearing a towel, or in a nudist camp, how do you know who's boss and who's employee? You can no longer distinguish social classes by external appearances. You can only distinguish people by their behaviour, by the details that most intimately reflect their personal identity.

In *Polygraph*, nudity isn't connected to the narrative; characters aren't naked because they're taking a shower or making love. Nudity appears through the bars of a police line-up; this resembles Eadweard Muybridge's photos of mostly naked people or animals moving in front of a grate he had placed against a wall. This procedure, by the way, was central to the birth of cinema. In fact, *Polygraph* is largely about making films, which helps to explain the visual references, since the narrative itself offers no logical reason for the people to be naked. When they are, though, they're liberated, having shed their respective social envelopes of waiter, actress and medical examiner. After we've seen them going about their business fully clothed and supported by props, we see them doing the same thing with nothing to define their status. And this helps us to move beyond the social level of the story.

It's not mere coincidence that modern dancers often wear minimal clothing or are entirely nude. The Montreal troupe La La La Human Steps, for example, use total nudity and even magnify it on a giant screen. And I think that, unconsciously, at a deeper level, it's an evocation of the gods. The body of Louise Lecavalier is the body of a woman with a man's musculature. Is there a greater mythological object than this fusion of masculine and feminine characteristics? And does anything define La La La Human Steps more than its physical presence? The same thing could be said of Marc Béland, who has worked with them and is a highly feminine actor with an extremely well-developed male body.

Nudity has something to say to the public. It can have an eroticising effect on the audience, of course. But aside from that, it's touching to see a naked person on stage. Too see an old man on stage wandering nude through a dark forest, as in Gilles Maheu's *La forêt*, is very moving and takes on a meaning beyond what you see. This kind of nudity isn't erotic. It emphasises a finality in life, the road the body travels towards death. In my father's last days before his death, my brother, my sisters and I had to help him with all his needs and every time he moved. We had never seen our father naked before. So these were special moments, shy moments, that made clear to me how far our morals and our mores distance us, separate us, from our bodies. It was very late for us to be learning about our father in that way. I think if we had learned this earlier we would have had a better understanding of who he was.

Some kinds of nudity are more expressive than others, simply because of the people we see on the stage. Doesn't the context in which nudity is presented also have a role to play?

An example that comes to mind is Marie Brassard's Lady Macbeth in the Shakespeare Cycle. Marie has often found herself naked in our shows, to the point that it's become a joke among us. But it's not that we do it on purpose and it's not gratuitous. There's always something in the play that requires it, like, for example, Lady Macbeth's madness. We see her nude at the opening when she's preparing herself for her husband's return, but especially later when in her madness she tries to remove the king's blood that she still sees on her hands. Until the previews in Maubeuge, in the north of France, she wore her big dressing-gown open as she walked on to the stage. But it wasn't working. As a joke I said, 'It's because you're not completely naked.' She laughed, but then she considered doing the scene nude and decided to try it. Everything was turned on its head. Suddenly, we saw the character without her Queen's costume, reduced to her simplest form. She appeared in all her fragility and the abnormality of the situation was all the greater. You have to be able to imagine the impact it would have had on the castle servants to see their Queen wandering about naked, talking to herself. It would have been a staggering sight for them. This is how nudity becomes much more than simply a question of revealing breasts and genitals.

In *A Midsummer Night's Dream* in London, a similar thing occurred. The play revolves in part around the conflict between King Oberon and Queen Titania over a little boy, who is orphaned at birth, adopted by Titania and who occupies all her nights. Traditionally, the young prince is played by a boy of eight or ten years old, sitting on the stage with tights and a little hat, and Titania makes Oberon jealous by coddling the young boy. But when reading through the play and seeing how the mother had died in childbirth and how the child had occupied all the Queen's nights, it occurred to me that he must still be a baby. The actress who played Titania didn't agree because she thought that, if he were a baby, there would be no sensuality to justify the jealousy and the conflict. But I see the relationship between a mother and her newborn as very carnal. In the scene in which the fairies sing a lullaby to the Queen and her little prince, I suggested Titania breastfeed the child. It was hard to convince her, but when she finally revealed a breast, the impact of the gesture was quite powerful. Her costume was entirely black and her skin was white as milk. With her exposed white breast feeding the baby, the audience could grasp all the sensuality, all the erotic pleasure expressed in the act of offering a breast to a newborn. There was nothing gratuitous in this kind of nudity; it added a lot to the very heart of the play, and suddenly justified all of Oberon's jealousy.

This story brings out the relative importance of nudity in different cultures. In London, a naked breast is a lot to ask, whereas in France, for example, total nudity isn't a problem. When *Polygraph* was performed in Hong Kong, we had a hard time getting the play's heavy dose of nudity accepted. In Japan, they had a different problem. It's not so much the sight of genitals that bothers them but the possibility of seeing pubic and underarm hair, which is considered the height of vulgarity. The actors had either to shave or to wear g-strings. So issues of context do exist on stage and depend on the specific requirements of a play as well as on the relationship with the audience.

Is there a connection between nudity and other demands of the production that might put the actors in a vulnerable position or in physically difficult situations?

Yes, there's a connection, but I have to point out that I don't make it my principal goal to create difficulties for the actor. Edouard Lock asks the impossible of his dancers in La La La Human Steps. Marc Béland told me that they sometimes throw fits, and even break a bone to prove that a particular movement is impossible. But they always end up doing the requested movement successfully and take pleasure in doing it because they defy the limits of the human body. I admire that. But, for my part, if I ask an actor to take up a challenge, it has to be within his capabilities. Even in Strindberg's *A Dream Play*, which was very physically demanding with the rotating cube and its angled surfaces, I always made sure the actors were comfortable. It's not a question of compromise for me. You can't treat everyone the same way, make the same demands of them. If an actor can't do a particular movement, the ball is back in my court and I have to find a new way to accomplish what I want.

If moving about and sitting on a steeply inclined platform is a difficult physical challenge for an older actor, just having him do it is enough for me. And when he does it every night, he's proud of it. Each performance, he accepts the challenge and that's what counts, regardless of how difficult the gesture would be for me or for a more athletic actor. What's important is the sense of transcendence. *Needles and Opium* taught me just how fit I would have to be for the show. I had to work out regularly in the gym to get to the point of being able to create the impression of flight. I had to lose some weight too. Working in a harness created a lot of problems for me at first. Since I'm a bit of a hedonist by nature, I have to discipline myself to accomplish these things, which is what I'm doing at the moment in preparation for my next one-man show *Elsinore*. I have the feeling it'll be a physically demanding show, so I'm starting to train now so I'll be able to transcend my limits.

That's what theatre is about. That's what the sport of theatre is. Our fascination with the Olympics has nothing to do with our interest in such and such a sport, but rather with the desire to see human beings transcend their limits;

to see someone dive, for instance, as if stopping time, delaying the moment of hitting the water for as long as possible by doing perfect figures in the air. Every actor has to have a physical challenge to meet: for an acrobat, it might be doing a backward somersault sixty feet in the air and landing on a tiny wire; for someone else, it might be sitting on an inclined platform. When you're aware of the challenge, the Olympian nature of theatre, the human beings on stage acquire a kind of nobility, a divinity. Our goal is Mount Olympus – not a gymnasium in Athens, but the place where the gods meet. The danger that actors and directors often fall prey to is forgetting this call to transcendence. It's a question of humility. We have to become aware that the texts we deliver, the characters we incarnate are greater than we are.

CHAOS

About ten days before the scheduled opening night of A Dream Play *by August Strindberg at the Dramaten (26 October 1994), Johan Rabaeus, in the important role of the lawyer, fell during a rehearsal and fractured two ribs. A decision had to be made quickly. The opening was postponed to12 November. For Robert Lepage, however, a three-week time-lag wreaked havoc in an extremely tight work schedule that ordered his days virtually to the hour.*

The administration surrounding the director and those with whom he was expected to work quickly responded. Dates were changed not only for A Dream Play *but for Michael Nyman's opera,* Noises, Sounds and Sweet Airs, *in Tokyo; for* The Seven Streams of the River Ota *in London and Paris; and for filming* The Confessional *in Montreal. In the midst of it all, Lepage flew to Ottawa to receive the National Arts Centre Award from the Governor-General of Canada, only to find himself, on his return to Stockholm, caught midair in a heavy storm.*

This sudden turbulence in the director's life, which at first seemed such a difficult blow, was soon transformed into a breath of fresh air and even a new source of inspiration. He confided as much, at any rate, on 8 November 1994 in a Japanese restaurant in the Swedish capital.

The dejection we experience when a timetable is upset is the very thing that helps to initiate change. No one is happy, for example, to see an actor get hurt. But on the whole, these moments are also a source of relief for me.

87

Our timetable involved a very rigid sequence of dances around specific problems, and everything fitted into a very precise, very well-ordered, rhythm. When something like last month's accident happens, it gives me ten days to do something else, and ten days as well to those who work with me to find other solutions, other ways of proceeding. Especially since the participation of a new actor, whether temporarily or permanently, forces us to rethink everything that was done before. Everything breaks down, then the pieces are reassembled and I finish gluing them together when I get back.

Many people want to regulate and tame the theatre. The theatre is something wild, without rules, that they want to prevent from growing naturally, organically. For me, unruliness of this kind feeds my work, like an unexpected rainfall. The day after the accident, Sonoyo Nishikawa, the Japanese lighting designer working on *The Seven Streams of the River Ota* as well as on Nyman's opera, taught me something. Like many Japanese people, she is extremely systematic and organised and I thought we would quickly lose her because of our rather chaotic manner of working. I generally saw it as an obstacle to our collaboration with the Japanese. However, when I was most depressed by all these unexpected disruptions, she told me that what interested her most in working with me was precisely the chaos I generated. I'm not really sure if I'm the one who creates it, but there is a fair amount of it around us.

Chaos is necessary. If there is only order and rigour in a project, the outcome will be nothing but order and rigour. But it's out of chaos that the cosmos is born – the order of things, yes, but a living, organic, changing one. This is where true creation lies. And here was Sonoyo, just when I was feeling depressed by all the upheaval, telling me that being decentred in this way was just what inspired creativity in her work.

We had this conversation over breakfast just before rehearsal for *A Dream Play*, in which my first task was to give the team a boost and some energy. Sonoyo's image of chaos served me well that morning because we were supposed to rehearse the first scene, in which the Daughter of Indra wakes up on earth in the company of the Glazier. And the very first question she asks at the moment of her human incarnation is, 'Why do flowers grow in manure, in mud?' Beneath this image is the Buddhist evocation of the world as a lotus flower blooming in stagnant water, in other words, in disorder and impurity. And the whole play speaks of the dust and mud from which this flower is born, of the suffering and chaos from which beauty and creation emerge.

These two moments did a lot to reassure me about the chaos that has always reigned in my life, the chaos that envelops my work. It gave the chaos meaning. A huge upheaval forces people to find new solutions, to reflect on how they might make it through. Working on *The Seven Streams of the River Ota* in London, I noticed that the entire focus of this work revolves around the chaos created by the bomb and what it engendered: beauty, life, and so on. The two extreme incarnations of World War II, the atom bomb and the concentration camps, both resulted in utter chaos. The art of war, especially the concentration camps, is composed of strictly organised acts that leave behind immense disorder. This kind of extreme organisation – creating lists, for example, of all the works written by Jews in order to destroy them and, in this way, destroy the very idea of a Jewish people – this organisation is completely contrary to the process of creation that comes out of chaos.

The outcome of this highly organised thing, war, is experienced in chaos, and it embodies the end of many things: the end of a way of life, of belief, of loving, the end of certain forms of society. It's in this sense that the idea of the Hiroshima bomb naturally leads us towards the idea of renewal; the idea of death towards the idea of sensuality and life. There is in death – it may seem terrible to say, but it's nevertheless true – a deep sensuality, a profound fulfilment of carnal reality. That's why *The Seven Streams of the River Ota* is a project about sexuality, a play in which sexuality is omnipresent. It deals as well with death, obviously. But the story of Hiroshima isn't just about a bomb being dropped and killing people. It's also the history of those who lived there before this event. It's the history of those who decided to live there after the bomb, to repopulate the city and give it life. And this is deeply sensual. Death is present, but not merely as an agent of pathos.

When I went to Japan for the first time in 1993, I visited Hiroshima with a guide, who, I learned on the last day of my visit, was himself a *hibakusha*, a survivor of the bomb. He had seen the bomb explode with his own eyes. He explained that the first things to be rebuilt in Hiroshima were two bridges. The city was built on the seven streams of the river Ota, and so it was important to re-establish transport links. But what's interesting to note is that they built a Yin bridge and a Yang bridge, one with phallic shapes and the other with vaginal shapes. For life to return to Hiroshima, they had to provide the city with sexual organs so that one half could couple with the other. There are superb views over the city from the surrounding mountains. At night, with the bridges covered in car lights, you would think you were witnessing a seminal exchange. Many of the anecdotes I was told in Hiroshima had to do with seduction, beauty, life. This is why all our attention was focused on the instinct of survival and on sexuality as an element of fecundity.

In *Polygraph*, death is also an important theme that is constantly linked to sexuality. One of the characters is a

EAST MEETS WEST IN A FLASH. Although his first solo show *Vinci* was concerned mainly with the Italian Renaissance, Robert Lepage showed his taste for things oriental even then: the tie he wears in this picture bears the inscription 'kamikaze', an odd resonance with the theme of suicide which was central to the show.

FROM A DIFFERENT PERSPECTIVE. *Circulations* was the first large-scale hit for Robert Lepage, and it was also a play where he first put to use some trademark moves. For instance, shifting the perspective so that the public sees events from 'above'. Here, the same scene was played twice in sequence, first from a normal perspective (*top*), then as if the moon were observing it through a skylight (*bottom*).

SHADOWS AND LIGHT. While it remained a local success, *A propos de la demoiselle qui pleurait* was remarkable for Lepage's accomplished use of lighting to define complex atmospheres.

VICTORY OVER THE DRAGONS. To this day, *The Dragon's Trilogy* remains the most successful work directed by Robert Lepage. Once again showing encounters between East and West, this time through the Chinatowns of Canada, the play showed a deep sense of ritual, as well as a capacity to capture the essence of daily life.

DEATH IN VENICE. In *Tectonic Plates,* Robert Lepage and his associates turned to the relationship between Europe and America, and between the nineteenth and twentieth centuries. The spirit of Delacroix and the physical presence of Venice were two driving forces of the show, as seen in the picture to the right.

THE SIDE EFFECTS OF OPIUM. In his second solo show, *Needles and Opium,* Robert Lepage turned his attention to the various causes of altered states of mind, including the drugs taken by Jean Cocteau and Miles Davis, the failed relationship of the main character and, as in the picture above, the effects of hypnotism.

FROM REHEARSAL TO STAGE. With *The Tempest*, the most successful part of Théâtre Repère's Shakespeare Cycle, Robert Lepage introduced within the Shakespeare play the idea of a play's creative process by gradually shifting from the setting of a rehearsal room (*above*) to a fully costumed production (*below*), giving a new twist to the often perceived relationship between Prospero and the author of the play.

DIFFERENT DREAMS. In three stagings of *A Midsummer Night's Dream*, Robert Lepage shifted his scenic design considerably. From a rotating island of steel in Montreal's 1987 production to a muddy pool in London in 1992, he opted for a wooden stage which opened to reveal a deep pool of water in his latest version, in Quebec City, in 1995. What remained was a very athletic Puck, played by contortionist Angela Laurier (*top*) both in London and Quebec City.

IS BIGGER BETTER? For Robert Lepage, both opera and rock concerts represent heightened and amplified forms of the theatre. Over the years, he has shown as much ease in one as in the other. When *Erwartung* (*top*) and *Bluebeard's Castle* first opened at the Canadian Opera Company in Toronto, he had young crowds lining up for tickets, just as they did all over the world for Peter Gabriel's *Secret World Tour* (*below*).

forensic surgeon. While dissecting a corpse, he explains how the flesh is made, how the blood circulates, how the various organs function or no longer function. The details are insignificant. What's important is that he has both his hands physically immersed in a body.

When you want to bring out the yellow in a painting, you use black. When you want to make a musical theme stand out, you use counterpoint. The same thing goes for themes in a play. If you want to reveal life and the instincts to survive and reproduce, you often have to approach them through death. *The Seven Streams of the River Ota* is entirely centred on this contrast. Nothing in this century represents death, nothingness and desolation as much as the atomic bomb. And yet, for us, it inspired a very living, extremely sensual show. Over time, I've learned that the recurring appearance of death and suicide in my plays has produced the opposite effect, that it has led us towards life. In a context in which death takes on so much importance, only those endowed with the survival instinct will truly stand out.

If you want to stage the birth of a new world, built on the ruins of an older one, you have to portray the world in ruins to make this transformation explicit. Cocteau says at the end of *Needles and Opium*, 'One world will end, another will begin. Americans, it seems that you will decide whether we have darkness or light.' Everything remains open. In 1949, he saw clearly that the United States would dominate the second half of the century, would decide whether we had war or peace. In his mind, we had to live through this war of massive destruction, of holocaust, genocide and the atomic bomb. The war had led many people towards darkness, but for Cocteau the outcome of world conflict provided instead an opportunity for rebirth from ashes.

If chaos is creative, is there not still a limit? Are there not moments when this type of disorder becomes too much, too difficult to sustain, even if only physically?

Around the time, in 1989, when I directed *La vie de Galilée* at the Théâtre du Nouveau Monde, in Montreal, there was a point when the energy I spent wasn't balanced by the energy my projects brought me – because of the way in which the projects were accumulating, but also because I let my energy dissipate defending certain ideas that should have been thrown away or else defending my reputation. But as a general rule, I rarely get tired in my work. The adrenalin I get from one project feeds the others. Constraint and disorder act as stimulants.

If I were to point to a particular difficulty, it's that the demands of large companies or film projects like *The Confessional* can take away from the time I devote to my personal projects. The number of people involved in the film, for example, made scheduling all that much more difficult. It's my personal projects that are closest to my heart. But it can be very difficult to set aside the necessary time to see them through because of so many external demands. It's a constant balancing act, and one that I still need to improve on. But, on the other hand, there's no question of fundamentally changing my habit of working on several projects at once. In my mind, it's a little like Leonardo da Vinci's countless involvements that kept him alive and kicking until a ripe old age.

The turbulent and fluid character of my work resembles the training of a body-builder. People often find body-building over-the-top or even ridiculous. But body-builders say that the descent into pain generates an energy that is addictive. It's genuine energy, created by excess. At times, I feel that my own energy comes from excess.

The Québécoise actress Pol Pelletier, who's now in her

forties, recently said in an interview in Quebec's theatre journal *Jeu* that she has more energy today doing extremely physical theatre than ten years ago, when, to all intents and purposes, she was conserving her energy. As we age, I think we have to be extremely active to stimulate our brain and all its unused nooks and crannies. We only use a tiny part of our grey matter in day-to-day life. We need to maximise this use.

We conceive of discipline in terms of rules and repetitive patterns. But, if we look again at body-building, we notice that this discipline requires surprising the body, not letting it fall into repetition. We train a certain group of muscles one night, another group the next morning, then skip a day and do three sessions the day after. Muscle-strengthening results from a routine that is constantly broken. That's what stimulates the body's energy and enables it to transcend its limits. The pain that comes with creation, with thought, is similar to the pain of body-building. The pain of a broken routine is a beneficial pain, and that's as true for physical muscles as it is for imaginative and creative muscles.

NUMBERS AND LETTERS

The number seven is the number of spirituality, the number of accomplishment, which connects the sky and the earth, the spirit and the flesh, in other words the number of harmony. So, on the seventh day, Sunday, God saw what He had created and rested. It's the moment when we rejoice in harmony.

Seven is also four plus three. And four is the number that represents humanity. The square and the cube represent human invention, the way humans organise the world, architecture. If you find cubes and rectangular boxes in my sets, it has a lot to do with my desire to structure space, to make architecture out of it. The circle, on the other hand, is the earth, the cycles (like that of the seasons), time, and so on. The symbol used to represent Quebec's participation in UNESCO is a cube inside a circle. The symbol of Real World, Peter Gabriel's company, is the square (civilisation) and the circle (the world in which we live).

Religion and spirituality, in almost all cultures, are represented by a triangle, by the number three. It's the Holy Trinity of Christianity, of course, but triple elements are everywhere. The meeting of the square and the triangle create a church, a meeting ground for the earthly and the heavenly, a contact between humans and God. You could say that about the Parthenon. *A Dream Play* tells the story of the descent of the Daughter of Indra into the world of humans. So I represent the world with a cube: the sites Strindberg uses are human places like the theatre or the home. But the cube we use is made of three walls, half a cube. And the grotto that represents Indra's ear, where all the prayers and complaints of the world converge, appears with its walls inclined at forty-five degrees so that the whole takes on a triangular appearance. Through its shape, the set tells of the meeting between the world of the gods and the world of human beings.

We're not talking about superstitions here, but about mathematics and symbols, just as we speak of the rules of spatial organisation. We know, for example, that there are rules about where an actor should stand on stage to create the greatest effect. It's also true in film: even if you put the principal character of the film in a crowd, the viewer will find him, as long as he's in the right spot on the screen. Clearly defining the surface of your canvas allows you to paint well. The same thing goes with numbers.

We have *The Seven Streams of the River Ota* and *The Dragons' Trilogy*; and *Vinci* was based on the number four. There's always a number in our productions. *The Confessional* operates around the number two, around the whole idea of duality: two periods, two brothers, the two bridges that connect Quebec City to the south shore of the St Lawrence, a new one and an old one, and so on.

The night I met Peter Gabriel, when he came to see *Tectonic Plates* was also the night of my birthday – the twelfth of the twelfth. The next time we met, we had started working together and he invited me out to a restaurant. Right there and then, he calculated on a paper napkin the number in numerology that corresponds to my name.[5] His is seven and he was sure that mine would be seven too, which it was. When I checked with the actors in *A Midsummer Night's Dream* at the National the next day, I saw that twelve of the fifteen actors also had seven as their number. Moreover, seven is the number associated with the Japanese goddess of the theatre.

What was even more astonishing was that, when we were working on the *Trilogy*, before deciding on the music for the show, we had improvised our scenes to Peter Gabriel's soundtrack for the film *Birdy*. The music had a lot to do with how the show evolved, and so I told Gabriel that he had, without knowing it, been an inspiration for the *Trilogy*. He was pleased to hear this, but, more important, he explained that since *The Lamb Lies Down on Broadway*, he has developed all his shows according to the I Ching and the principles of Yin and Yang. And the I Ching was one of the principal work tools in the *Trilogy*'s development.

The other night, at home, I decided all of a sudden to find an anagram for my name. My work has created such expectations these days that I sometimes tell myself it would be interesting to see what reaction the public would have to one of my shows presented under another name. On a whim, I got out a game of Scrabble and, playing around with my name, came up with 'Peter', which left over 'Gabroel as a surname. The difference is a single letter, an 'o' for an 'i'. You can go a long way with this kind of a crazy connection. You could say that because our anagrams are similar, because our number is the same, we were meant to work together, that in fact I'm Peter Gabriel's double, and so on. It's like the people who try to find hidden meanings in Shakespeare's name. I find this fascinating. It's not so much that I believe in it, but that it's a kind of poetry that helps me to create. Maybe the connections are only made because we decide to give meaning to the games of numbers and forms. But even if we don't understand why they exist, these connections are nevertheless there.

The numbers and symbols emerge on their own. The

number of the flight that falls into the sea at the end of *The Dragons' Trilogy* was calculated by Marie Michaud. She didn't want us to choose it randomly because numbers always seemed to take on a meaning in the show. So she calculated a number – 384 – which somehow fitted perfectly. You have to understand that the show was developed in three stages: an hour-and-a-half (half of three), three hours and six hours (two times three). The six-hour version was first performed in Montreal on 6 June, the sixth day of the sixth month, in hangar number nine. The date wasn't chosen by us but by the Festival de Théâtre des Amériques. Even if none of it has much to do with anything, really, these are like guidelines that give meaning to our ideas.

At the start of the Hiroshima project, we worked with the number twelve: the twelve months of the year, the twelve signs of the Chinese horoscope, travelling to twelve capitals and through twelve time zones. But the rules of the number twelve weren't working all that well, and the number seven emerged as the right one instead. Since then, the number has haunted us; we see it everywhere and it really sustains the show. It's not the *Seven Streams'* lucky number. It's a tool that helps us give a poetic order to the show, like the dragons' colours or the Yin and the Yang did.

This kind of poetic order doesn't only appear in new creations. At one point in Strindberg's *A Dream Play*, the Poet and the Daughter of Indra find themselves in Fingal's Cave. They have just been in a church, and the notes of the organ are transformed into human moans and then the church itself is transformed into the grotto, which is Indra's ear, the place where all human pleas are gathered to make their way to God. Strindberg had written a lengthy essay showing that the dimensions of Fingal's Cave are the same as those of Notre-Dame in Paris and explaining the connection between the two places, a connection that, according to him, wasn't accidental.

We don't lead our production to a given place. We let the production guide us there. We try not to force our ideas, our concepts, on to it; the show has its own logic, poetry, rhythms, that we have to discover. This is as true for a newly created work as it is for an established play. One of the big failings among theatre directors in the second half of the twentieth century is their tendency to impose elaborate and very detailed directorial plans on their plays from the start. Each new directorial idea has to be neutral enough to allow the meaning of the play to emerge on its own.

18 January 1995, Quebec

In addition to this whole mechanism of numbers, I often hear people who work with you say – you do, too, in fact – that when you find a point of entry, a theme that sustains the show, the theme starts to crop up everywhere. But it can't all be of use. How do you filter all this information?

You have to distinguish between what is truly dramaturgical material and what is merely recurrent. During our brainstorming sessions to find a title or while determining how to use a particular idea, we end up seeing some things emerge repeatedly. So it all depends on the way we approach our work. In *The Dragons' Trilogy*, we determined what we'd keep and what we'd eliminate by resorting to I Ching every once in a while. It provided us with the image of a well, which involves digging, seeking out the roots, the heart of things. So we understood that our characters had to dig inside themselves to find their own roots. From this one idea, character development became very important and everything surrounding the characters was relegated to the background.

Improvising around a source idea, an idea for a scene, leads us down all sorts of paths. Sometimes it'll be a very little thing that we'll have to look at more closely in order to be able to uncover its meaning. So some scenes will become absolute microcosms of the show, holograms of a sort, each particle containing the complete image of the object being presented. A little detail of what might crop up in the process of creation might suddenly reveal the kernel of the show and help us create a kind of order. In *The Seven Streams of the River Ota* there's a scene in which a cultural attaché from the Canadian Embassy and his wife invite a Québécoise actress, on tour in Hiroshima, out to a restaurant. We created the scene in a single improvisational session which we videoed, transcribed and then left almost untouched in the show. For us, it was a fun scene, but we didn't really see it as being more than entertaining, a series of good lines. When we showed it in London in the fall of 1995, a few actors who came to see the show told us how fascinated they were by the scene. We were surprised, but as we discussed it, we realised that the actress served as a vehicle for many essential things in the show: relationships between art and life, aspects of human sexuality, etc.

Some scenes have an organic quality to them. When you feel good about a scene, it's often because its chemistry conforms well to that of the show as a whole, even if it's not immediately obvious in the subject matter. You shouldn't ignore this feeling since it's a good guide to how to create a show. Marie Gignac pointed out to me when we improvised a scene in *Seven Streams* that it was the first time since *Trilogy* that we had kept a scene that had been formed in a single take. The entire *Trilogy* was made that way. We always knew what we needed. We would improvise it once and most of the time it stayed just as we'd done it. We would correct a few details in later rehearsals, but the essence would fall into place right away, maybe because the *Trilogy*'s story revolved around things that had a personal resonance for us – our mothers, the Quebec City of their and of our grandparents' youth. Similarly, the restaurant scene in Hiroshima, portraying the encounter of a Québécoise actress on tour and a cultural attaché from the Canadian Embassy, resembles what our lives have now become.

CREATION

THE FLYING MACHINE

Since Robert Lepage's international career and productions are unique in Quebec, it would be safe to assume the same of the organisation that makes them all possible. Often neglected in discussions of Lepage's creative process is the important role played by the 'shadow' side — logistics — in the creation of the 'light' side — the productions themselves. Yet this shadow side has been a central aspect of Ex Machina's development: over the last few years, much of the company's energy has been devoted to the creation of La Caserne (a former fire station), a multimedia production facility located in the historical centre of Quebec City. Comprising a black box theatre and film studio as well as recording and multimedia facilities, this centre opened in early 1997, ending a long period during which Lepage often felt a little homeless, especially with regards to a production base. The setting in which we spoke of the complexity of Lepagian logistics exemplified this feeling perfectly: on 19 September 1994, after an entire day of meetings devoted to his various projects, our conversation took place in a taxi on the way to Stockholm airport, from where he was to catch a flight to Paris, as he did every weekend, to work on the editing of his film The Confessional.

1 always find it a little odd to be in transit between two places of work. But it's well organised this time and that's encouraging. Working with large companies makes travelling and accommodation easier. With the help of the Japanese, the Swiss or the French, we can hold meetings all

over the world. We still organise some of the meetings ourselves, but less often now, since we work increasingly in partnership with others.

We can now say, 'On such a day, we will all meet in such a place', no matter if it's Stockholm, Paris or Montreal. And everyone will be there: the Japanese lighting designer and her assistant, the Québécois set designer, our Montreal, London and Paris agents, and so on. And the more we take on, the more we want all these people to be intimately connected to each other. This is an important element of the Ex Machina project. We're now in the process of opening offices in various cities. It's still quite modest – a telephone somewhere in somebody's office – but doing this has helped to develop, and even made necessary, a greater intimacy between us and those who, at first, were only business associates or occasional co-producers. They've now become members of Ex Machina, in a way.

Over time, a kind of natural selection has taken place among members of the team. There's no implied judgement here of the people who didn't stay the course. It's simply that they needed a different kind of stimulation. The people who stay tend to be stimulated by the prospect of navigating in virgin territory, of experiencing this type of supreme stage fright. For example, opening night is generally a kind of culminating point for actors, when problems have finally been resolved – at least, as often as possible. But for us, everything can be turned upside down between the dress rehearsal and opening night. So the opening becomes a kind of discovery, a single moment in the evolution of a show. And if we're not trying to reinvent theatre each time, it just doesn't excite me. Some actors are completely overwhelmed by this approach; others are happy only when challenged in this way.

Philippe Soldevila, my assistant, and Michel Bernatchez,

previously the administrator and technical director of
Théâtre Repère and now of Ex Machina, as well as Jean-
Pierre Saint-Michel, my agent for over ten years now,
have all agreed to work without a safety net. They have to
be inventive, and come up with their own ways of working. We never argue and no one says, 'This is the way to
do it.' Instead, we decide collectively how to proceed. The
division in arts companies between artistic direction and
administration is often too hermetic. Everyone excels in
his or her field, but there's no cross-pollination. No one
has any influence on anyone else. Sometimes, you'd even
think that the different sectors worked for different companies.

Our creations and methods of working are quite idio-
syncratic and we have to be very imaginative in the way
we administer everything. Philippe Soldevila is an unusual
assistant director, who probably deals more with the logistics of my work than with its artistic content. Jean-Pierre
Saint-Michel was the one behind the creation of Robert
Lepage Inc., the company responsible for hiring all the
personnel for my personal projects, including me. The
company allows us to co-ordinate my personal contribution to my own projects, but also to invest in different
projects when other producers lack a sense of adventure.
Robert Lepage Inc., and the people it employs, is still a
primary investor in Ex Machina.

Michel Bernatchez has a special gift for this kind of
administration. This is essential to artistic creation since
one of the fundamental problems I see in a lot of theatre,
at least in Quebec and Canada, is the tendency to prepare
all theatrical dishes in the same way. Some shows only
need two minutes in a microwave, others should simmer
for an hour. But the need for different recipes is never
acknowledged: it's always three weeks of rehearsal in
English Canada and six to eight in Quebec. The system is

a little bit more flexible in Quebec, but it's still bound by the rules of the Union des Artistes. Although the Union's mandate is to ensure artists aren't exploited – which is important in itself – its rules can't always be applied to all forms of theatrical expression because they are so rigid. The plays of Brecht or Shakespeare or Chekhov might all follow a similar recipe, but each also requires a very specific approach. And people in production circles are rarely aware of this.

I have to say that we have the luxury of not depending on ticket sales as much as most theatres do. Our company doesn't have to start its season by a particular date with a Molière play to guarantee a full house every night. Sometimes we have very tight deadlines – our schedules are perhaps too tight – but, as a general rule, we have the luxury of being able to attend any given festival with a show that's only partly developed.

Michel Bernatchez has always been able to define and shape the technical aspect of whatever project we're working on by focusing on the artistic content and then adapting his own work to the particular challenges of the creation. His influence on the work is enormous. More than anyone else, he has the authority to intervene if problems arise in my absence, to make artistic decisions and get things back on track. From the start, at Repère, Michel would look at what was envisaged for a show and would find ways of adapting the technical support to the demands of the work. Even if he's kept very busy with accounting and logistics during the day, he regularly comes to see what we're doing in rehearsal and his opinion carries a lot of weight during our work meetings. His artistic judgement is extremely accurate and he's taught us a lot. There was a point at Théâtre Repère when the number of projects going on simultaneously made it difficult for him to be able to follow them all assiduously, but with Ex Machina his responsibilities are more focused, and he can devote more of his time to the content of the shows.

Michel Bernatchez doesn't deal only with problems and finances, although a good part of his work often consists in saying no, in telling us when to stop. Mostly, he's the one who asks if the game is worth the candle. Sometimes, he'll look at a project and say that it doesn't justify the degree of technical complexity we've developed. In the first stages of *Polygraph*, he warned us that our staging was overly elaborate given the project's diffuse nature and that, as a result, the audience wouldn't get it. It took us a long time to work out the problem. But touring a production acts as a filter; it forces you to simplify it technically, and ultimately this helped us to create a better show. When we started working on *The Seven Streams of the River Ota*, Michel decided that, this time, he would put no technical or financial limits on our creativity. But this creates a different problem. A third of the way through the project we found ourselves with fairly elaborate and heavy set and stage machinery to drag around. We had to make use of all these resources, and to think of how to continue using them all in the future stages of the project. So we have developed methods to accommodate our way of working and to make the machinery serve the story we are telling.

The way in which we work has a strong influence on our day-to-day lives and creates needs that we wouldn't necessarily have anticipated. For example, in developing *The Seven Streams of the River Ota*, we realised we would probably need a cook because of our long working hours, our many trips, and so on. Our operation is becoming a little like a circus or those old-style itinerant theatre troupes, with their caravans, masses of luggage and everything else. All the paraphernalia of the circus might seem like mere decoration on the surface, but it reflects the underlying reality of the work. It tells you a lot about how the artists live and how their art transfuses their entire way of life. Given all this, until recently, the big piece still missing from our operation has been a proper work space, which we will have in La Caserne: a centre tailored to our needs, where we can work at our own pace and in conditions that suit us.

These changes have a lot to do with your international career taking off, of course. Weren't there several stages, though, an initial set of tours for the multinational projects?

One of the results of the way my career took off was that the collaborative nature of our work was forgotten. It might be hard for people to understand this. In contemporary theatre, we tend to see the director as the person responsible for a show. But what initially drew me to the theatre was precisely its collaborative nature. Being shy and timid, I found in theatre a way to undertake artistic work with other people.

That's why it was hard for me to find myself so closely scrutinised by the cameras. In 1989, I reached a point where I couldn't hide behind a company any more. If my name was associated with a project or a production, even only indirectly, it was my name that made or unmade it. My name became bigger than the group or groups I was working with. Everything became personal and my shows were no longer seen as being the shows of companies with which I was involved. I no longer had the protection that belonging to a group had offered me at first. And the credit I received was often out of proportion with my real contribution. I know that I'm not the only one this has happened to, but it was dizzying nevertheless.

When I became artistic director of French theatre at the National Arts Centre in Ottawa, things shifted somewhat for me. It was the first time that I actually took over the full direction of a company. In other words, for the first time, I took on the role that was being attributed to me anyway.

Things get more complicated once you start dealing with technical issues and differences in human and financial resources within a growing and increasingly international company. At the beginning, a big hall for me meant two to three hundred seats. I had never thought I could fill six hundred, eight hundred or twelve hundred seats. The challenge with *Needles and Opium* was all of a sudden to do a one-man show for eight hundred to a thousand people, whereas *Vinci,* for example, had been put on at the Théâtre de Quat'Sous in Montreal to an audience of fifty. How do you maintain a sense of intimacy with a thousand people? You have to rely on technology to magnify you, to change the scale on which you work. With *Needles,* we were successful in creating a sense of intimacy in a big space and in general it works quite well. But, all the same, I can no longer perform in either Quebec or London in front of twenty-five or fifty people, even though that's often precisely what I would like to do. To do that now I have to come to places like the Dramaten in Stockholm. Here, in the tradition of typical Swedish chamber theatre, great actors can play to houses of fifty people, in tiny spaces, but with sufficient resources to do a professional show. The budget of *A Dream Play*, on which I'm working now, is four times bigger than the annual budget of the Théâtre du Nouveau Monde in Montreal, and, yet, the play will be performed each night to between one hundred fifty and two hundred people. That just doesn't happen in Quebec.

Similarly, I'm always astonished to find myself in a big national theatre where I have to pretend to be someone who normally works in a big national theatre, when I still work for a little Quebec company. You always have to adapt to the relative levels of investment, technical means and human resources. We're now realising that in order to develop partnerships with all the big companies we've worked with we have to make Ex Machina bigger. Two or three people in an office just isn't enough any more. Everyone has assistants and even the assistants have their assistants. We work with project designers, special collaborators, and so on. And we're discovering how important it is to generate resources with an initial project that will then feed subsequent ones.

I have to say that production costs also depend on the venue. The set for *La Vie de Galilée* at the Théâtre du Nouveau Monde in Montreal was the most expensive set of that theatre's history. But the show also brought in record ticket sales, so it ended up balancing out. But if we had built the same set at Théâtre Repère or even now at Ex Machina, it would probably have cost a third of the sum. Some things cost an arm and a leg, not because I have expensive taste, but because the costs are exorbitant in the places we want to produce our shows. And this is often because of a lack of appropriate means and the lack of a strong theatre tradition in Quebec.

We deal with such wide variations of scale that it's difficult really to take in the differences. The annual budget of the National Theatre of Bavaria in Munich, where I worked on a collage of Shakespeare plays, is equivalent to the total sum of government funds devoted each year to theatre in the province of Quebec– that entire amount to produce twelve shows at the Munich theatre in an atmosphere where, on any given night, they can simply decide not to perform for any reason they might consider valid. When I was planning the set I had in mind for the show there, they called my assistant Philippe Soldevila the day after receiving my fax to say that if I wanted to fly out the following week, they would build the proposed set with me there and adjust it to my specifications. The show was supposed to start five months later and we didn't understand what they were talking about. But it's a standard procedure there. They call it the *Bauprobe*, a kind of set rehearsal. You inspect the prototype and tell them, 'The door is too small', and they get out their power-saw and make it bigger. I spent two days there and could have gone back again over the next few weeks if my schedule had allowed it.

When Robert Wilson plans his shows in Germany, he can spend two weeks designing the lighting. Just the lighting! Whereas, in both Repère and Ex Machina, we have rehearsed shows such as the cycle of three Shakespeare plays in six or eight weeks, and done everything during that time, from the acting to the lights to the sets. And we perform at the same international festivals. We don't have the means to work like Robert Wilson, Ariane Mnouchkine or Giorgio Strehler, yet we compete in the same festivals, we get the same media attention, we face the same critical expectations, we're considered to be of the same calibre. When you rub shoulders with artists like these and their administrations, you see just how vast the difference is. How can you compare the three Shakespeares we did four years ago with the production of *A Midsummer Night's Dream* in London, which was done with human, technical and material resources we could only dream of at Repère?

At first, when we toured internationally, we were pretty much a Québécois and Canadian theatre troupe. All our collaborators were Quebecers, or almost all. But this won't last, unless we're suddenly given the means to become a Quebec company of international calibre, so that we can create our own equivalent to the National Theatre of Bavaria. To be able to meet present needs, we have formed international partnerships. Our current productions clearly reflect this fact. This echoes Brook's situation: he is based in France but doesn't actually represent France, partly because he's not French, but also because his actors come from all over the world. We're increasingly becoming a company of this kind, one that can't be defined in strictly national terms. In *The Seven Streams of the River Ota*, we work with a Swiss-German soprano, Rebecca Blankenship, with a Japanese lighting designer, Sonoyo Nishikawa, with French collaborators, and English Canadians. To be able to work at the international level today, our creative as much as technical and financial collaborative efforts have to be international.

I agree with Denys Arcand in a sense when he says that we ultimately achieve the things we deserve to achieve, that we get the things we hope for. One might even say that our talent corresponds to our ambitions. If a young director wants to direct plays in an established theatre, with decent funding and twenty-night runs, it's probably what he'll end up doing. Becoming artistic director of an established theatre will be a kind of zenith for him. If we want to create shows and tour them internationally, we'll also find the means to do so. Of course, Ex Machina already has access to co-producers in most places throughout the world. We've developed exceptional partnerships. But this is also connected to what we want to do, which is export our shows. If your ambitions have a local focus, what you end up with has a local focus. It might sound pretentious, but it's true. If an actress dreams of performing regularly at the Théâtre du Nouveau Monde in Montreal, when she gets leading roles there, she gets what she's deserved. Denys told me, for example, that Geneviève Bujold wanted a house in Malibu and she got her house in Malibu. We achieve these things thanks to a certain amount of luck, a certain amount of talent, to happy coincidences, at the cost of certain lifestyle choices and through lots of work. I've always wanted to travel, to get to know other countries, even before I had my first local success. So my life took shape accordingly.

AFTER THE REHEARSAL

The dynamics of a play, whether you direct it twice or sixty times, remain fundamentally the same. Each time you direct it, you emphasise or you de-emphasise certain essential aspects of the play. Sometimes, you get carried away with the idea that the play is mostly about one particular theme, but often, you're completely wrong. So you try again another time and you look elsewhere. But with each new try, you know a little more than the last time.

Take Dutch painting. What makes a Rembrandt painting rich is its accumulation of quite different superimposed layers. It becomes a little like a colour photographic plate, on which the pigments of three primary colours are set successively, so that the overall effect is achieved through layering. The colour chemistry in Rembrandt's paintings follows a similar procedure. For example, he might paint a first image entirely in shades of red, then work with other series of colours. The viewer doesn't see the red but can feel its effect on the top layers. So the same subject is painted in five, six, seven layers before you even get to the final product. It's not just pasted on in one throw.

That was the impression I had when I directed *The Tempest* in Tokyo, having worked on the play four times before. I wasn't at square one any more. I'd already confirmed some of the ideas I'd had about the play's essence. Once a director has established certain ideas, certain interpretations, he can direct accordingly, and the actors have something solid to rely on.

I don't like the way some directors impose strict or overly defined conventions on their plays, nor the way others need to sign their plays in a very obvious and personal way. When a director puts on *The Cherry Orchard* or *Julius Caesar*, it's often 'his' *Cherry Orchard* or 'his' *Julius Caesar*. I find it very difficult to have to deal with these sorts of expectations. When I put on my collage of Shakespeare dream texts at the National Theatre of Bavaria, the artistic director was expecting precisely that kind of distinctive and immutable signature, and he walked out of the dress rehearsal completely dumbfounded, saying, 'Why didn't you create the same production as your *Midsummer Night's Dream* in London? Why is this so different?' The reason is that I don't yet have these texts under my skin. At first, when we work on a play, we embroider, we find gripping images, and so on. Then, we gradually work towards the play's essence and it begins to take shape. People might think that when we redo a play we add totally different elements or give the play a new meaning. What we are really doing is working in layers on the same object to make a more complete picture each time. It takes time and many new opportunities.

The ideas of directors like Peter Brook, Bob Wilson, Peter Sellars, Giorgio Strehler, Peter Stein often come out of previous experiments in their studios, ideas they had the opportunity to explore before directing the play and signing it in a definitive way. But for a Quebec director these kinds of explorations are practically impossible. If you want to survive, keep a company afloat, work here alongside other Quebec and Canadian companies, it's impossible. So you have to choose the other path, and return to the same text as often as possible. I hope that one day, after six, seven or eight tries at *The Tempest* I'll be able to find the right framework for the play, and do a definitive production, having finally learned what it's about. It's a huge undertaking, which you can't do with only six or eight weeks of rehearsal, and in a single go. And, of course, not everyone has the privilege of being able to go back over something.

Does the audience need to understand this particular method of creating?

It's not really the audience that needs to understand our method of exploration, of trial and error. It's the critics. The audience wants to be entertained. They pay, they want to get their money's worth and go home having felt or learned something. Critics, though, have to learn to take time to absorb what they have seen in a show and then must either recommend it or advise the public against it, explaining how they reached this judgement. This requires both a good understanding of the work and a good appreciation of what the public knows.

No one believed in what we were doing when we planned to stage *The Dragons' Trilogy* in three successive versions. Since Quebec City's population is so small, no one believed that people would go to see the same play three times. But it worked. Not only did people come to see the three versions, they often came back two or three times at each stage. People aren't forced to take part in the process. They're invited to come and see the results. They either accept the invitation or they don't, depending on their evaluation of a company.

Since Quebec has a very young repertoire and very few prolific playwrights, the only Québécois plays we can remount within a company's lifetime are the plays of Michel Tremblay. In a country like Sweden, a single company might easily perform fifteen or sixteen versions of the same Strindberg play. In France, people rarely come to the theatre to discover *Tartuffe* or *The Imaginary Invalid*.

They've seen them too often before. So, in those countries, theatre has acquired a kind of museum status which
hasn't yet happened here.

*Do you have to make certain adjustments to allow for the differ-
ent expectations of audiences here and in Europe?*

You have to keep your eyes open and stay alert. I think,
for example, that our decision to do the Shakespeare Cycle
was poorly understood by French-speaking critics in
Quebec, whereas this wasn't a problem elsewhere in the
world. The simple fact of putting on three of these plays at
once was an event in Quebec, because the French community here doesn't really know Shakespeare's plays.
Putting on Michel Garneau's translation of *Macbeth* to an
audience of fifty in Montreal and having the Montreal
theatre journal *Jeu* write about it doesn't mean that people
will understand what it's all about. Critics compare, draw
analogies, talk of other productions, other ways of produc-
ing plays, other interpretations. It's interesting for the
theatre milieu, but it's completely useless for the public at
large because they rarely understand or have first hand
knowledge of what's being discussed. And the idea behind
presenting several Shakespeare plays at once in Quebec
was precisely to make his plays known to the public. We
have a lot to learn from these plays, but this fact is rarely
reflected in media coverage. I often repeat something the
theatre critic Robert Lévesque once wrote: he suggests
that we shouldn't underestimate the public's intelligence,
but neither should we overestimate its cultural knowledge.
It's a great line, but I find it's used in an odd way.

*In this respect, aren't your productions and interpretations of plays
more naturally accessible to audiences who know these plays and
who might be able to make comparisons?*

No. If you start by thinking that the audience will understand everything, will have full knowledge of the facts, you have a problem. Fundamentally, Quebec audiences come to see shows and discover new plays. That's all the more reason we should put on three Shakespeares at a go. The audience needs to see as many plays as possible, however they respond to them. In Quebec City, Shakespeare is essentially never put on, and in Montreal, if a *Hamlet* or a *King Lear* hasn't been successful, we have to wait another five or ten years before we see it again. Directors who put on a classic from the world repertoire for the first time in Quebec face a different problem: if it isn't produced according to certain canonical rules, it's often poorly understood. Sometimes it seems we have to wait for the play to be remounted before it can achieve the freedom it needs.

People rarely read the classics in Quebec, and we don't put them on often enough here. Even critics have to go elsewhere, like London, Paris or Stratford to get to know the world repertoire. If the theatre community really wants to educate the public, we have to apply ourselves, to show them the great plays as often as possible.

When we produced the three Shakespeares at Montreal's Festival de Théâtre des Amériques, the troupe was exhausted, the shows didn't work that well, things weren't running smoothly. But our houses were full to bursting and the shows were well liked. So what we planned to do succeeded in part. But it would have been even more successful in front of a much larger audience, in large outside settings such as the Parc des Îles in Montreal or the Plains of Abraham in Quebec City, for example, because the ultimate goal was to have the French-speaking public discover a repertoire that it virtually never gets to see.

Here we come back to the notion of museum status I spoke of earlier. In my opinion, we have to see plays by authors from around the world again and again, and specifically here in Quebec we must see even more by Québécois writers. At the moment, we're not doing the necessary groundwork to create a strong national repertoire because we don't remount plays already in existence. We have to exhaust the present repertoire, to re-experience constantly so that it really does become a repertoire. A few years ago, works by Québécois playwrights Claude Gauvreau, Réjean Ducharme and Marcel Dubé were remounted, but this was only for a short time, whereas we should be constantly coming back to these authors so that they become truly established in our culture.

This is a key to understanding why we constantly need to justify the theatre's existence in Quebec. No one questions the existence of a museum because of a bad exhibition or a controversial decision. When the National Gallery in Ottawa bought Barnett Newman's *Voice of Fire* or exhibited Jana Sterbak's meat dress, the scandal aroused focused on the museum's acquisitions policy, not on its very existence. But a Quebec theatre company that puts on a few bad productions can easily see its existence questioned. Even the Théâtre du Nouveau Monde in Montreal hasn't yet achieved this museum status which it should be able to claim as its own. In my opinion, this has a lot to do with our lack of an established repertoire; there's nothing in the fridge.

SOUND AND LIGHT

During our first series of conversations in Stockholm in September 1994, Lepage always took a break on Sundays and Mondays from his work directing A Dream Play *to fly to Paris for the editing of* The Confessional. *After a full autumn of commuting, the next phases of postproduction in the winter and spring brought him to London and Montreal. Our last conversations in Quebec City took place at the beginning of May 1995, on the eve of the film's première at the Cannes Film Festival.*

Given the timing, we could not ignore the topics of Lepage's début as a film director and film-making in general. Probably because his career until then had been more intimately linked to the stage than to the screen, these film-related topics tended to crop up while we were discussing other themes. They were often the result of comparisons drawn between the different art forms with which Lepage has experimented. When considering the crucial contribution of the various visual and sound technicians, who 'make or break a film', Lepage wondered if 'the work actors do between being handed a script and a final performance – precisely when the theatre triumphs – plays as big a role as it should in film'. And so a discussion of the two pillars on which film is built, sound and light, naturally led to a consideration of their place on the stage.

This relationship between stage and screen has only recently become a more active preoccupation. Robert Lepage's second movie, Polygraph, *is an adaptation of a stage-play which was greatly reworked to become a cinematographic work. Meanwhile, video images have crept up in ever more active ways in his latest productions,* Elsinore *and* The Seven Streams of the River Ota. *The first section of this latest collaborative work is in fact entitled* Moving Pictures.

LIGHT

Our discussions of the function of light revealed that Lepage and another multidisciplinary artist, Laurie Anderson (with whom Lepage had come into contact through Peter Gabriel's company, Real World), shared certain similar concerns. During the spring of 1995, Lepage was impressed to find in Anderson's most recent book, Stories from the Nerve Bible, *a section on technology as a gathering place for modern societies, replacing the camp fires of old. This very same idea had emerged earlier as a starting premise for one of our talks in Stockholm in November 1994.*

Fire is always what brings people together. In the great black of the night, we gather around a fire to tell each other stories. Fire is used to inaugurate important events: the Olympic Games are opened with the lighting of a torch, which, however, does not illuminate the whole stadium. Fire is the symbol for gathering. When we assemble in a cinema and are plunged in darkness, the light is restricted to the screen. It's like watching a fire, a light whose shapes and colours are in constant motion.

The light connection is profoundly mythological. Every year since the fifteenth century, the Japanese have held Noh theatre festivals, festivals of light held at night, in which they light huge bonfires to illuminate the stage. Whether you consider it an art form or entertainment, the purpose of the festival is to celebrate light. And working in film has confirmed for me the importance of the notion of gathering, because light is the primordial condition of its existence.

In film, we identify with the characters, and the importance we accord any given character is directly connected to the number of seconds he or she appears on the screen. In theatre, on the other hand, what we are drawn to are events, rituals over which the characters officiate. I don't really know how to explain it, but in *The Dragons' Trilogy*, for example, although we do sometimes identify with the characters, their history doesn't move us as much as does the place where the action occurs and its relation to time. If necessary, theatre can exist without light, but not film, which, ultimately, is an account of what happened to the light in a particular place at the time of filming. All that gets imprinted on the plates is light. The actor, in film, is only a luminous impression. Or more accurately, the actor is a luminous impression that is outlined, magnified or reduced.

Twice, when we were preparing to shoot *The Confessional*, I was offered as a gift what's called a director's finder, a series of adjustable lenses that help you determine what frame, what lens and what space to use; in other words, to decide how best to have the light pass through the camera. Film is defined by this tool. It's microscopic, literally as well as figuratively. It's like a magnifying glass that scrutinises people's minds and words. In film, you either pull back or zoom in; it all comes down to proximity. You can't do this in theatre. But sometimes people get bogged down trying to do a kind of analytical theatre, trying to make the audience see what you need a magnifying glass to see, when really theatre is an art that proclaims things, that shouts out its message, so that it can be heard all the way to the back row. Theatre seen through a magnifying glass is imperceptible, except in the tiniest of spaces, such as in chamber theatre. I like the choice that film gives me. But some subjects are best seen with a magnifying glass, others from a distance. So some are better dealt with on the screen, others on the stage.

SOUND

Given his reputation as an 'image-maker', Robert Lepage's move to film seemed a natural step. Moreover, the Cannes critics unanimously praised his remarkable technical mastery as a first-time director. However, with the sole exception of his use of light, it was not so much about images that he spoke during our conversations, but rather about the importance of sound to both his film-making and his work for the stage.

People often speak of the 'cinematographic' aspect of my work, and everyone who has encouraged me to do film has done so as if this were my medium *par excellence* because of the visual qualities of my plays. However, I see film as a medium of writing and sound, whereas, to me, radio is the real medium of the image because the listeners have to create their own pictures. I've always wanted to be a radio host. In high school, I had a lot of fun doing radio and even skipped class in my last year to hang out in the student radio station. More recently, when I came up with the idea of staging *The Tempest* in a rehearsal space, it was mostly to work out how to create images without gadgets and costumes. Having actors use tables, chairs and everyday props to evoke the magic of the play was one approach; but, ultimately, the best way to solve this problem is to do a radio play, to let the listeners create their own images. I don't think I'd ever turn down an offer to write a play for radio.

Film-editing has taught me that what really shapes film is sound. People go to see images, images and more images, of course, but what would these images be without sound to unite them, to bring them together? Watch the opening credits of Louis Malle's *Lift to the Scaffold* without Miles Davis's music and what's left?

Bergman said that film is a three-dimensional thing: sound is the first dimension, image the second, and the meeting of the two creates the third. Because silent film has no words, it has no dimension. Sound tells you what to look at. Let's say we were shooting this scene. While you look at your tape recorder, I want to attract people to my glass. By tapping the glass with my finger, I draw everyone's attention to it. It's the sound that does the work, but paradoxically, a sound-track is successful if it's discreet. It was a great discovery for me to hear Denys Arcand explain, during an editing session for *Jesus of Montreal*, that 'Sound's greatest virtue in film is to go unnoticed.'

The same connection to sound exists in my stage work, too. The skaters' waltz scene in *The Dragons' Trilogy*, in which soldiers on skates act out the destruction of the war by scattering groups of shoes representing families, would not have the power it has without Robert Caux's music. The same thing applies to many of the scenes in *Needles and Opium*.

Aside from music, the power of *Needles* has a lot to do with the resonance of the text. People react not only to what Cocteau says, but also to the way he says it. The rhythm of his words reflects what it is he's saying. This is also true for Garneau's translation of *Macbeth*, which finds its real musicality in Shakespeare's words. I believe the text an actor speaks is music. Dramatic literature is strong when it's musical, when we're forced to speak the text in a non-natural way, almost to sing it. This is Shakespeare's strength: the resonance of the text reflects what is being told, reflects the mood of the characters. The *Elsinore* project has a lot to do with revealing this musicality in Shakespeare's writing and what it can tell us about the meaning of the text.

Working in opera has stimulated my thoughts on the subject. In the theatre we're often handicapped by our search for a subtext. We can spend hours searching for what's hidden in a scene, in a line. But in opera, the subtext is the music itself. That's where you find the work's meaning and, even if actors are stiff on stage, the show will quickly take on an energy and power because of what the music conveys.

THE REALITY OF THE
CAKE PAN

Robert Lepage's stage productions are most frequently described as
'works-in-progress', a notion that, at best, is imprecise. Seeing a
show as an object in constant evolution, which is an essential com-
ponent of Lepage's work in the theatre, has spawned many queries
and much criticism, often boiling down to the same question:
When can we say a show is 'ready'? Drawing on culinary
imagery, the director replied, on 9 May 1995, that it all comes
down to the baking, to the pan you choose and the dough you pour
into it.

Because of our way of working, we face what I will call the
reality of the cake pan. For example, if we do a two-hour
show, a comedy, we need a small angel-cake pan, quickly
filled, quickly cooked. But for a seven-hour saga like *The*
Seven Streams of the River Ota, the pan has to be much bigger. When you pour the 'mixture' in, it's obvious that,
until it touches the sides, until it fills the pan properly, the
cake won't rise and the result will be rather thin.

A show doesn't have to be complete to be performed in
public, and in any event shows grow throughout their run.
It is important to reach a certain stage in the level of development and this is different for each production. Some
shows do well being developed and presented in stages,
others less so. When people found our shows too thin and
superficial, it wasn't because we had nothing to say, but
rather because our material hadn't sufficiently taken shape

at the time they saw it – it was still at an interim stage; we were still building on it in the lab.

In the case of *Seven Streams*, we obviously shouldn't have presented it as it was for the first time in Edinburgh, in such an official context. It was the Festival that chose to open with our show and to put it in a big 800-seat space, when we had envisaged a 200-seat space, a smaller event. But we should have settled for putting on a kind of public workshop, a series of the best elements developed in the first stages of rehearsal, which also would have allowed us to discuss our method of work with the public. Michel Bernatchez was right to lengthen our rehearsal timetable scheduled for the winter and spring of 1995 to fit in public rehearsals. This allowed the mixture to reach the sides of the pan just about all the way round and thus begin to rise nicely in spots.

In future, when we're creating a show, we should not undertake an obligation to show up at a big première on a given date. This is where La Caserne will play an important role. It won't be exclusively a theatre – it will be more like a factory where we will develop our work in a controlled environment. Our way of proceeding with *Seven Streams*, given all our mistakes and the show's evolution over the course of the spring, has only confirmed our decision of several years ago to create Ex Machina. And, in fact, the company works on the same culinary principles, but now our pan is the whole planet, and includes a multitude of disciplines. We'll need a lot of dough to fill it.

PARADOXES

FREEDOM AND SLAVERY

But freedom starts with slavery and
sovereignty starts with dependence . . . It
would seem that I need to be dependent
to know finally the consolation of being
a free man; and it's certainly true.

Stig Dagerman, *Our need for consolation*

*The notions of freedom and constraint appeared in two forms in
our conversations: first – on the light side – when the idea of the
theatre as a place of metamorphosis somewhat mysteriously trans-
formed into a paradox found in Shakespeare's* The Tempest; *then – on the shadow side – when we discussed Robert Lepage's
work with Théâtre Repère. It was there that his creative spirit was
able to find its own voice and free itself, before the company generated a feeling of imprisonment. As with many of his ideas,
freedom is manifest in the life and art of this artist in both its
shadow and light aspects – two sides of the same coin.*

THEATRE TAKES SHAPE IN FLIGHT

One of the traits people notice and appreciate most in your dra-matic work is the way in which people, places and objects are transformed in full view of the audience, so that they take on a new appearance or meaning. What makes this device so impor-tant?

People come to the theatre, often unconsciously, to wit-ness a transfiguration. On one level, this might take place in the simple act of seeing a young actor play an elderly character. His voice is transformed and his facial traits are changed through make-up, etc. But there's also another more spiritual level of transformation that takes place when an actor is inhabited by a character – or a character by an actor, depending on your perspective. Finally, we find transformation within the narrative itself: throughout a play, characters are put to various tests that cause them to undergo metamorphoses. Plays that endure or, at any rate, those I'm drawn to, are often those in which we find some form of transfiguration: *Macbeth*, Strindberg's *A Dream Play* or even, more literally, *A Midsummer Night's Dream*, in which we see Bottom transformed into an ass.

These transformations are at the heart of ritual. In the Catholic Mass, for example, the priest transforms the bread and wine into the body and blood of Christ. This is exactly what the ritual of transformation is all about: the entire Mass converges on this moment of transubstantiation. In fact, one of the first lines in *The Confessional* is taken from this moment in the liturgy: 'This is my blood, the blood of a new and lasting covenant.' The film begins, therefore, with a ritual or, more precisely, with the funeral rite of Pierre Lamontagne's father. And throughout the film, we follow the transformation of Pierre into his brother Marc, a transformation whose dramatic importance is largely brought out through physical change. It's what we have come to see, in the end; we wonder what will become of the character, how he will change.

This phenomenon exists in all of literature, of course. But in theatre, the transformation is not explained to us – we witness it. Take Strindberg's *A Dream Play*: the play's action covers a century. Some characters remain unchanged throughout the century, others age ten or sixty years in a day. Ultimately, the whole play revolves around the changes wrought by the passage of time. I'm very drawn to plays in which the characters are transformed, but also to plays in which the sets are transformed and matter is transcended. It's incredible to be able to travel through time and place, to infinity, all on a single stage. It's the metamorphoses brought about on stage that make this kind of travel possible.

You're quite insistent about the concrete aspect of these transform-ations: sets that move, characters who change physically. The meaning of a play, its substance, often seems to appear quite liter-ally in the objects we find on the stage. How do you draw the play's meaning out of such solid and mechanical props?

Too often, I think, we try to exploit themes or explain things to the audience, rather than simply telling the story, letting what is unfolding on stage do the work. I think that if I remain fully aware of the stage as a place of physical transformation, I make it possible or can try to make it pos-sible for the audience to really feel the direction in which the action and the characters are being hurtled: literally – because a set might turn in on itself; or figuratively – because of the way we might choose to tell the story and stage it. So rather than just being a mode of working, the transformation becomes the whole basis of the work. Sometimes, people ask me, 'What do you mean here?'

Perhaps it would be better to ask, 'What is happening here?' I find that what people most notice on stage is the action. It's the action that holds their attention when they're in their seats, and that's what will lead them, when the show is over, to understand what is hidden behind it. So I think that even when they've seen a more obscure, more difficult play, the audience can still easily grasp its essence and be moved. You have to let the show take shape on its own, let the meaning emerge freely.

Even though it might seem contradictory, sometimes freeing the meaning can also involve constraining the actors with very precise instructions. This paradoxical relationship between freedom and constraint is a fascinating aspect of artistic creation, which my work on *The Tempest* revealed time and again. For the longest time, I was very unhappy with the version I was directing in the Shakespeare Cycle. But in the end, it became the strongest of the three parts of the cycle. By the time we got to Tokyo in November 1993, I could finally take pleasure in the show. And I noticed that several great kabuki actors, who had performed the play themselves, cried while watching it because they had understood the freedom of our production, because the meaning of the play seemed to emerge with such clarity. But if it took a long time to achieve this effect, it's because of the paradoxical way in which freedom manifests itself.

It was largely Peter Brook's production of *The Tempest* that put me on this trail. The first scene, which is the tempest scene itself, was an extraordinary experience right from the first moment, and very demanding for the actors. But after, I found that the intensity dropped a little, that the overall effect was much more conventional.

In the Preface to Jean-Claude Carrière's beautiful translation, Brook said that the key word of the play is 'freedom' and, in fact, Prospero's final word, and the last of the play, is the word 'free'. When you reread the play with this idea in mind, you see that the whole play speaks of slavery and freedom: people vowing to free others, free themselves, or even to become another's slave. So Brook concluded that he should free the actor, and he set his production on an empty stage, with virtually no props.

I had read the play some time before coming across Brook's ideas, and I'd thought to myself that it should be set in a rehearsal space where the actors would read the text and improvise scenes. What a hellish nightmare that was! Nothing worked. The actors were generous, they tried things out, but they weren't improving from one performance to another. They would constantly ask me to block them, to give them precise directions. But I refused, telling them simply to play to their heart's content, to let themselves go. They were obviously capable of it, having done it in rehearsal. Why couldn't they do it in performance?

In spite of everything, the idea seemed to go over well with the audience. In general, *The Tempest* was the play that got the best reviews among the three. Whether people liked our Shakespeare trilogy or not, whether they liked the plays or not, people seemed to appreciate the principles underlying the production of *The Tempest*. In my mind, this appreciation can be understood because the concept finally came to be validated. And this was because we stopped improvising, because we made final, irrevocable decisions.

To create the impressions of flight, enchantment and wandering in *Needles and Opium*, everything had to be fixed from the start. To create the impression of transcendence, you have to be bound. You're far from being free: to fly, you need a harness and wire. And in *The Tempest* freedom came when we finally fixed everything very precisely. Once they were harnessed and directed, the actors could set themselves to freeing the substance of the play.

For the play's meaning to be freed, the actors had to be imprisoned.

PRISON OF DREAMS

> Dreams become reality (and then you're
> stuck with them).
>
> Robert Lepage, Notes from his
> sketchbook,
> London, November 1991

When we got out of the Conservatoire d'Art Dramatique in 1978, Richard Fréchette and I were the only graduates not to be hired by a professional company. So after a three-week workshop with Alain Knapp in Paris, we founded our own company, Théâtre Hummm... The name came from an onomatopoeic line that constantly recurs in a well-known French comic strip by a cartoonist called Fred. In January 1979, we put on our first show in a bar. It was called *L'attaque quotidienne* and was all about the daily tabloids. We started at the end because people reading these papers often begin with the back page. Our shows were based on collective improvisations and on observation, methods that were fashionable at the Conservatoire and in much of the Québécois theatre world.

Among our most exciting exercises at the Conservatoire were our observation days: we would go out into the city to find a character from everyday life – even animals in a pet shop – and we would come back to improvise on the

A NEW POINT OF VIEW. Robert Lepage tries to see the world through a director's finder (*top*), during the filming of his first movie, *The Confessional*. The movie builds on an underlying tribute to Alfred Hitchcock's *I Confess*, which was also filmed in Quebec City, and whose storyline also relied on events revealed to a priest during confession (*bottom*).

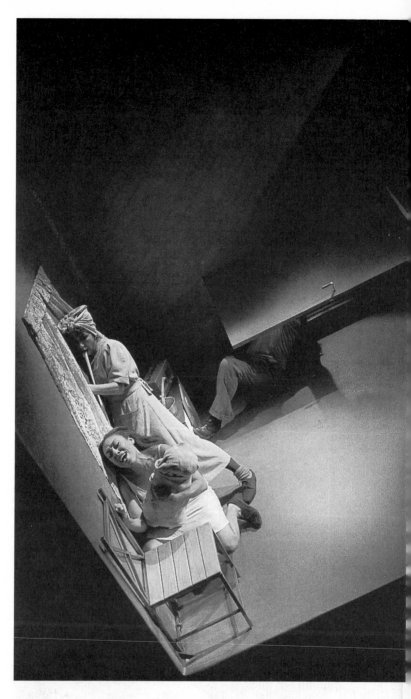

PLAYING WITH A DREAM PLAY (*above and opposite page*).

In Robert Lepage's version of Strindberg's classic presented at Stockholm's Royal Dramatic Theatre (in rehearsal, *above*), the set was essentially a large open cube representing the world of man which Indra's daughter has entered. Thanks to a motor and a three-ton counterweight, the cube elegantly rotated to indicate the passage of time, throwing a house topsy-turvy (*facing page*) or becoming a street corner where an officer's love remains unrequited (*bottom right*).

THE VERY FIRST PICTURE. The picture above was taken during the very first public rehearsal of *The Seven Streams of the River Ota*, in March 1994. At the time, only two of the seven hours of the play had been put together. An expert in calligraphy was brought in to draw elements of the story which were to be taken over, at a later date, by the actors themselves.

AMBIGUITY AND IDENTITY. Relationships between East and West are at the core of *The Seven Streams of the River Ota*, where they coalesce in various ways. Here a Quebecer sits in a Japanese house in Hiroshima, a young man wearing a woman's kimono.

THE TRACES OF TIME. Making different times and places overlap on stage has been a trademark of Robert Lepage's directing. At one point in *Seven Streams*, several people sit in parallel times in a tiny common bathroom, which also serves as a photographer's darkroom, as though their presence were actually a trace of their past presence.

THE MANY FACES OF *POLYGRAPH* (*above and opposite*). Like all plays
directed by Robert Lepage, *Polygraph* constantly evolved. But the play
underwent a greater metamorphosis than any other as it became a movie
filmed at the beginning of 1996. The degree of change required for
Polygraph to pass from one artistic form to another is obvious in the treat-
ment given to scenes involving the polygraph or lie detector machine (in
the play, above, and, in the film, *top right*). Theatre (as well as opera)
made its way into the movie: two of the main characters start a relationship in a dressing-room, after a performance of Hamlet (*bottom right*).

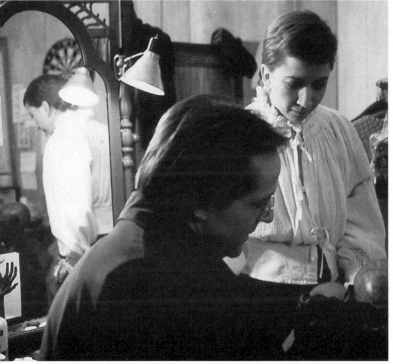

THREE IS A CROWN. In Elsinore, Robert Lepage plays all the characters of Shakespeare's *Hamlet*, thanks to much technology and great flexibility in acting different characters at once. For instance, in the opening scene (*above*), he successively plays Claudius, Gertrude and Hamlet, simply by shifting his position and his attitude on a chair where all members of the family sit under the weight of the crown.

character and create skits. *Saturday Night Taxi*, which we first put on in 1981, was based on that kind of observation. I have to say that it took me quite a while to move beyond the methods I learned at the Conservatoire, to stop doing shows that might please my teachers. That's one of the current problems in theatre in Quebec City: because the Conservatoire has taught us all so much, as artists we often have a difficult time freeing ourselves from our training to develop our own work. The principle that Marc Doré taught us, to find theatre in the things of daily life, was extremely liberating at first, but you have to be able to move beyond it.

In 1980, I was asked to direct a show for Théâtre Repère, which was called, ironically, *L'école, c'est second-aire*. Repère was based in the Quebec suburb of Lévis and had been founded by Jacques Lessard with Denis Bernard, Michel Nadeau, lrène Roy and Bernard Bonnier. It started off well but, a few successes aside, the shows weren't taking off. Apart from directing that show, I had no direct association with Repère before 1982. Richard and I had tried to join forces with them on several of our earlier projects because Théâtre Hummm... had no funding. But until 1982 it hadn't worked. What happened was that at the end of 1981, morale was very low at Repère, since they had practically no cash and they even worried they would lose their grants. So we suggested to Jacques that we do a show together with their few remaining dollars – which were more than enough for us. And we did *En attendant*. After that first successful collaboration, Jacques invited us to join Repère, and Théâtre Hummm... died a timely death.

En attendant, in a sense, united Jacques Lessard's creative theories about the Repère cycles with the intuitive method that we were using in our shows. Our understanding of theatre had a lot in common with theirs, and the Repère method provided a means for us to stimulate and elaborate our creative language. Being at Repère also gave more weight to what we had done before at Théâre Hummm... .

For each of us, though, the cycles represented something quite different and produced different results. Some were better suited than others to making use of the cycles as a creative tool – Jacques was more comfortable explaining than applying the method. In fact, for quite a long time, people tended to confuse the Repère method with its results. People tended to think that, if they followed the method, they would produce a Robert Lepage play – a belief which Jacques Lessard always tried to dispel when he gave one of his numerous lectures on the subject.

Repère was home to many great collaborations. For quite a while after we joined it, the company developed as Richard Fréchette and I had hoped it would when we'd joined, but we also became prisoners of it in a way. A dream can imprison you once it becomes reality: you hope an ideal company will take shape and run in a certain way, with certain goals. But when it comes into being, it's not necessarily as liberating as you might first think.

All of us – Jacques Lessard as much as Bernard Bonnier, Irène Roy or Richard and I – wanted to create a forum for actor-creators, not only for actors. Marie Michaud, Marie Gignac, André Jean, who all joined us early on, weren't there only to perform. André didn't want to limit himself to only one thing. He wanted to write, direct and act. For a while, Repère was the only multidisciplinary company in Quebec City. It was very daring. We were among the first to do improvisational competitions, which later became quite popular in the province. We were always on the lookout for new things. During our *Top Repère* evenings, we did stand-up numbers, but also performances based on poetry, music, and so on. A lot of ten-minute numbers were created during these evenings. They were later integrated into other shows or even became the basis for new shows.

In the beginning, Repère's vitality came from our strong desire to further our training. Being at theatre school offers the chance to explore new territory, which is very difficult to do once you're professional. Once you graduate, you are no longer allowed to make mistakes. Given that Repère was run by a teacher at the Conservatoire who liked to work in this way and that it attracted the graduates who learned more from open workshops than from scene studies, the company perpetuated the playful and experimental vein that the school had taught us.

During a class at the Conservatoire, Guillermo de Andrea had had us reading a line from Brecht that went something like, 'I left school because I had nothing else to teach my teachers.' Guillermo thought that Brecht was a little pretentious, but I found this idea really interesting. And in fact it gained new meaning several years later when I met Nicholas Negroponte, the director of the Media Lab at the Massachussets Institute of Technology, first at a conference on technology in Montreal and then at a dinner in England where Peter Gabriel had invited him to discuss a technological theme park project in Barcelona. Negroponte talked a lot about new technological developments and new approaches, explaining that some cultures were finally beginning to understand that teaching wasn't something passed on from professor to student, but from student to teacher. So, the computer is not only used to provide wholesale information to the student, but also allows the student to confront the computer's view of the world with his logic. And this enables a form of apprenticeship through dialogue. For me, directing follows the same logic. We have to question actors rather than answer their questions. And this approach profoundly alters the dynamic, although not everyone is equipped to play this kind of game.

We generally conceive of education as providing answers to questions that haven't been asked. The teacher gives out unsolicited information to the student, information such as the population of Canada is 27 million or Mount Everest is 8,846 metres above sea level. A good teacher is one who succeeds in arousing the student's curiosity so that he can actually want to know the population of Canada or the altitude of Mount Everest. The teacher creates a desire to understand. In the same way, the most interesting kinds of theatre trigger a series of questions in the audience, rather than simply providing answers.

Repère had this quality of asking questions about the theatre and encouraging the audience to do the same. But at a certain point, through everyone's fault, including my productions and those of Jacques or Bernard, Repère began to provide answers, to officialise, to offer as answers, as truths, what had formerly been only questions. And we all became more or less imprisoned by the company's style, by what people expected of us. Jean-Pierre Ronfard and the late Robert Gravel, the heads of Montreal's Nouveau Théâtre Expérimental, had to work round this dilemma. They had strokes of genius and other less fortunate moments, but I always liked their shows, even the less successful ones, because they retained an enormous freedom, the ability simply to say, 'It was a good question, but it didn't take shape' or 'It wasn't the right question'.

What allows the Nouveau Théâtre Expérimental to maintain its freedom is that it is a truly experimental theatre and its members don't depend on it for their livelihood. They earn a living doing TV or directing plays in established theatres, for instance. Repère couldn't sustain this kind of approach because very soon it became the primary source of income for its members. Repère is located in Quebec City, where there's no television or big theatre market to offer regular work. The stumbling block we faced was that while wanting to be experimental and to provoke and stimulate the public, we also had to earn a living. Even with good grants, we couldn't reconcile these two objectives.

If Repère was a training ground where Robert Lepage's language and that of many others gradually took shape it also harboured many conflicts. After several years, profoundly different approaches to research, to productions and to touring shows provoked a split between Robert Lepage's productions, which were constantly on tour, and Jacques Lessard's activities, which were principally based in Quebec City.

From *En attendant* onwards, Jacques Lessard, Richard Fréchette and I were being asked to perform in Montreal, but Jacques told us we shouldn't go, that it wasn't a safe bet, that we would be taken advantage of, and so on. We finally began to feel that he was a little afraid to leave Quebec City and to present his work elsewhere. When *Circulations* won first prize at the Quinzaine Internationale de Théâtre in 1984 among a very impressive international selection, offers came pouring in from everywhere in Canada. But still Jacques resisted touring around the country, arguing that we had other priorities. That's when Bernard Bonnier, one of the quietest guys I know, had literally to slam his fist on the table to say we had to go.

Touring *Circulations* completely redefined Repère's work, and launched the company's international career. That's when the ideas that later fed into *The Dragons' Trilogy* were born. Our travels from one end of the country to the other, and especially our time spent in Canadian Chinatowns, did a lot to inspire the *Trilogy*.

The problem was that the success of my projects took over and somewhat strangled Repère. Our priorities shifted to touring our shows, and the members whose work wasn't designed for touring were sort of shut out. Very soon, there were two Repères. At first, we saw this as an asset, telling ourselves that we had a local home-based division, involved in research and pedagogy and run by Jacques Lessard, and an international division, which generated the theatre's reputation, tours and funds. But these two divisions couldn't continue to live together and a serious conflict arose.

I left Repère once in 1987 because it just wasn't working any more and then I came back for a year because Jacques Lessard promised to change the company, to establish two legitimate divisions, a promise he had a very hard time keeping. Lots of people were important at Repère: Marie Gignac, Michel Bernatchez had established themselves there and had also tried to restructure the company to allow for these two distinct roles, but Jacques's approach made a genuine reorientation impossible. So, in 1989, I left for good and went to the National Arts Centre. Gradually, other members left too, and the company eventually died out.

The conflicts at Repère became a real thorn in the company's foot and prevented it from becoming what it might have been. And because of this, our dream for Ex Machina is that it will become the type of multidisciplinary and experimental company that Repère wasn't able to be.

THE CHEAT

In my understanding, the whole art of theatre revolves entirely around cheating – knowing when to trick the audience, when to cheat, and also when not to cheat. In life, we might ask ourselves where the line lies between making love with someone and screwing them. The same applies to the theatre: cheating is a necessary part of the game, but sometimes you can go too far. One of the criticisms levelled against the very first cut I did of *The Confessional* was that I had played too many tricks. I had thrown too much dust in the viewers' eyes. The editing was so convoluted that the plot wasn't clear. And David Putnam, the British producer, told me, 'Yes, you have to cheat, but the viewers have to feel at the end that you did it to entertain them.' When a director edits his plot well, we're happy in the end to have been led by the nose. Cheating is a risky art form. It can produce happy results, but also much less happy ones.

ENTRANCE EXAM

People may consider this to be a tribute, but it really was my sister Lynda who started me off in theatre. Ironically,

145

she herself never acted until I offered her a role in *The Confessional*. I think that this has something to do with the way we were brought up. The girls in the family had to adhere to stricter rules than the boys. I think that this pushed them to find some way of leaving home sooner to find greater freedom.

However, it's my sister who inherited our mother's instinct for performance, which I would love to have had myself, but which seems to have eluded me. For me, performance quickly became part of a much larger whole: very early I wanted to try my hand at set design, directing, inventing special effects. The actor's role for me was one creative tool among many. But performance comes quite naturally to Lynda. What it takes actors years to learn, she would master in a few minutes. She constantly astonished us during the shoot, and when we showed the rushes to the London producers, one of them even asked me for her agent's number.

She's also the one who introduced me to the work of Michel Tremblay and to the director André Brassard, who are sometimes a team and sometimes not. First, she took me to an amateur production, in 1972, at the Anne-Hébert School, of Tremblay's *En pièces détachées*, my very first play. One of her best friends, wrestler Tony Baillargeon's daughter, was acting in it. And because of that, they replaced a reference in the play to Johnny Rougeau, a famous wrestler from Montreal, with one to Baillargeon, the local hero, which, of course, always got a good cheer from the audience.

It was also Lynda who took me to see my first professional play at the Trident in 1974, where Brassard was directing not a play by Tremblay, but a French version of *Twelfth Night* by Shakespeare. The show sent shivers through me because of its inventive way of telling the story and because Brassard hadn't just put on the play, he had directed it, he had given it life. The show taught me what you could achieve through the art of directing. Brassard and Tremblay were also at the heart of one of the first films I ever saw, *Il etait une fois dans l'est*, a film by Brassard based on the world of Tremblay.

Unlike most people brought up surrounded by French culture, I didn't come to theatre through Molière, but through Shakespeare, Brassard and Tremblay. I didn't really even touch Molière until the end of my training at the Conservatoire, in a production of *Dom Juan* directed by Jean-Pierre Ronfard. He had divided the title role into two: the *Dom Juan* who travels and the one who stays at home, which I played.

The fact that I even made it to the last year at the Conservatoire was only thanks to my having tricked my way in. Having seen these plays and having performed for the first time, I decided that I wanted to be in theatre. So I started skipping classes more and more often to act. I was setting my sights on the Conservatoire and, when I looked into the requirements, I discovered that the week of try-outs, in which they chose candidates for the school, coincided with the week of final exams set by the Ministry of Education. Since I had essentially given up on my classes anyway, I knew that passing the exams wouldn't be enough for me to get my high-school diploma. So, rather than face the humiliation of redoing a whole year, I gambled everything.

To get into the Conservatoire d'Art Dramatique at the time, you had to have a high-school diploma and be eighteen or older. I didn't meet either of these criteria. But I put in an application anyway, and I put down my real age – which they obviously didn't really notice – and that I didn't have my high-school diploma. When they asked me about the diploma, I told them how important it was for me to do the try-outs and that I could sit the Ministry exams at a later date to get my diploma. And despite the fact that I had cheated, they accepted me into the screening process, which still astonishes me to this day.

I only realised how serious the consequences of my gamble really were when I found myself face to face with the 150 other participating candidates. Some had university diplomas, others had done a year or two at other theatre schools. Everyone was older than me and everyone seemed to know what they were talking about. And here I was, a little smartass who had only taken one or two high-school drama classes. I very soon became convinced that I would never be chosen. In my own mind, I obviously didn't have what it took and so I was the first to be surprised when they ended up accepting me. Maybe they realised I wasn't there just for the fun of it, that I really wanted to be in theatre. Anyway, I never heard another word about high-school diplomas.

During the next three years, I had some moments of great exhilaration, some long periods of discovery, but, on the whole, the experience was rather difficult for me. I couldn't do some of the things that were asked of me, probably because I was too young to understand them, but also because some teachers were real charlatans. Guillermo de Andrea, for example, no longer had much to offer, but he insisted on maintaining his authority. When I couldn't perform the way he wanted me to, rather than show the kind of generosity a teacher should, he would point me out as an example for the other students not to follow.

At the other end of the spectrum, Marc Doré profoundly changed me, helping me to discover poetry, which I knew nothing about: the poetry of the body, the poetry of space, of objects, of words. He was a genuine father figure to many of the students who have since become some of Quebec's finest actors, such as Rémy Girard, Normand Chouinard and Marie Tifo. Though it is little known, his influence on theatre in Quebec City and in Quebec as a whole is considerable. On top of it all, Marc looked like my father, which made my bond with him all the stronger. As soon as he saw a hint of poetry or invention in someone, he showed them a lot of affection and generosity. But I also detected some bitterness and disillusionment in him, which seems to me to be a common phenomenon among many people of his generation. I sometimes have the feeling that I'm the son of a bitter generation, of a generation – my parents' as much as my teachers' – that felt betrayed by its era.

Marc Doré was a student of Jacques Lecoq with whom he remained good friends; after he completed his training, he and two fellow students, Yves-Eric Marier and Normand Cazelais, committed themselves to a political, Marxist-Leninist, very hard-edged, kind of theatre. But when we were at the Conservatoire, the whole Communist movement was crumbling and many of its dreams with it, and our society was turning towards a materialism that totally contradicted the convictions of the Left. Lots of people from this group – militant trade-unionists, the first nationalists, Communists – remained very bitter.

Most important of all, Marc Doré passed on ideas he had learned from Jacques Lecoq, methods of discovering the poetry in things, of discovering how to tell a story, how to speak. You also find this among Lecoq's other students, such as Ariane Mnouchkine at the Théâtre du Soleil, and Philippe Gaulier, who carries on Lecoq's teaching in London and who, moreover, taught Simon McBurney and many others at the Théâtre de Complicité. In fact, it's through McBurney that I met Lecoq, in London, at the opening of their show *Street of Crocodiles*. Lecoq had also come to a performance of *The Dragons' Trilogy* in Paris, and was very moved to see students of his students, Yves-Eric and Marc, who were carrying on the Lecoq tradition.

THE NEIGHBOUR'S COPY

> One must stand before a masterpiece and
> copy it. Originality resides in the degree
> to which one doesn't actually succeed in
> the copying.
>
> Raymond Radiguet, quoted by Jean
> Cocteau in
> *Jean Cocteau par Jean Cocteau: entretiens
> avec William Fifield.*

When you bluff once and you get positive results, there's
a good chance you'll do it again and that you'll end up
being caught somewhere down the line. The cheating
caught up with me in 1987 when I was preparing the
French version of *A Midsummer Night's Dream* in Montreal.
I was in a rush and, when it came to writing a little text for
the programme I stole two great lines from Jan Kott's
Shakespeare Our Contemporary, exchanging a reference to
The Brothers Grimm for one to Walt Disney. It was a stupid trick, like copying from the exercise book of a fellow
student. The following November, in Quebec's theatre
journal *Jeu*, Carole Fréchette brought to everyone's attention 'her impression of *déjà-lu*', of having read the lines
before, and rebuked me for this appropriation. The following January, Robert Lévesque at *Le Devoir* read the
journal – other critics had probably also read it but not
made much of it – and he wrote that Carole Fréchette's
article had confirmed the impression of *déjà lu* he'd also
had at the time. The story then caught on in the media,
perhaps more than it really deserved. I'm not trying to justify or excuse what I did, but it was after all very peripheral

to my work and I was being treated as if I had plagiarised another author's writings for one of my own creations.

Having said this, it was neither the first nor the last time that elements in my work were blown out of proportion. When in 1990, Robert Lévesque – him again – announced in *Le Devoir* that I would direct *King Lear* in French at the Théâtre du Nouveau Monde in Montreal, he devoted a whole section of his article to questioning how someone who was still wet behind the ears could even dare direct such an important play. He stated that it made no sense to give me the job since I had hardly ever touched Shakespeare. He certainly got one thing right in his article: Olivier Reichenbach, who was then artistic director of the Théâtre du Nouveau Monde had in fact called to offer me *King Lear*. But our discussions hadn't gone beyond a telephone call. I had said no, precisely because I didn't believe myself up to tackling the play before having directed more of Shakespeare's other plays. So here I was being criticised for something I wasn't even doing.

To return to the question of plagiarism, I think it's a much more serious matter when an accusation of plagiarism is levelled against me for the tributes I pay to great artists by integrating their works into my own. Even before we had started to edit *The Confessional*, its fate was being decided in Montreal's *Voir* magazine. One part of the film's story is set in 1952, during the shooting of Alfred Hitchcock's *I Confess*, and so the columnist Georges Privet wrote a long piece on the parasitical practice of mining the works of geniuses, saying that people were now used to seeing me do it with artists such as Cocteau and da Vinci.[6] l was still shooting *The Confessional* when his piece came out. The film wasn't even completed – we were in the middle of the creative process. And even though the film actually refers to many other things, even though the allusions to Hitchcock are quite minor, here it was being evaluated and judged sight unseen.

I think people have a lot of difficulty distinguishing between borrowings, tributes and plagiarism, although there are, of course many grey areas between the three. I recognise a lot of my own methods in the shows of other artists, both in Quebec and elsewhere in the world. Usually, I'm proud of it, as long as it takes on a life of its own. I've never hidden the fact that my first shows were strongly influenced by the work of the Montreal director Gilles Maheu and his company Carbone 14, and Gilles Maheu isn't shy about saying that I've borrowed ideas from him. In this case, we're talking about a tribute, although there's a fine line, of course, between gratefully borrowing and actually stealing ideas.

It's almost become inappropriate to admire people. You can no longer say, 'I admire Hitchcock and I'll do what I can to make you love him as I do.' You can't do that. You're not an artist if you do that. It's astonishing that some critics consider this approach plagiarism and point a finger in this way when Quebec television is largely a pla-giarised version of American and French television and *Voir* magazine itself copied parts of its format from the French tabloid *Libération*.

We need to develop a sense of wonder, a sense of admi-ration that is not focused on ourselves, but on others, on things that surround us. A little before he died, André Malraux asked to have his thoughts recorded. He felt that he hadn't communicated everything that he wanted to and so he taped eight or nine broadcasts to express what he still had to say. He had throat cancer and so he coughed the whole time, but the series was brilliant. And when he was asked what he had most loved in life, the final thing he mentioned was his sense of having admired people, of having been awed by art. In his view, we live in a world in which people busy themselves seeking admiration, wanting to be told they are brilliant, rather than admiring what's around them. Preparing a meal – creating something that's pleasing to the senses – is a pleasure, but eating – where the senses actually enjoy the food – is the real pleasure. We live in a society that no longer takes the time to eat, but that nevertheless continues to make new dishes.

ENERGY AND EMOTION

At the Conservatoire, I was taught a definition of emotion, which I learned but never managed to produce on stage. And for three years, I was told that I acted without emotion. Right from my very first professional shows, however, I managed to move the audience. I didn't really understand what made this happen and it took me a long time before I began to sort it out, before I could really distinguish the difference between the emotion that an actor feels on the stage and the energy he needs to generate that emotion in the audience.

Marie Gignac explained to me one day that, when she'd been working with Jacques Lessard on *Fuente Ovejuna* by Lope de Vega, she had had a very difficult time doing a scene in which her character had just been raped. At first, she'd tried to perform the emotions, the pain of the character, but it hadn't worked. It was when she'd actually tried to generate the violent energy that comes out of being raped that it had all finally fallen into place for her.

You have to know how to control and channel energy, to create outlets for it, to put up blocks when necessary, to allow it to overflow, but mostly how to hold it in. This is the kind of thing I started to learn during my three-week workshop with Alain Knapp. Knapp, a Swiss, had worked quite a bit with some of Brecht's contemporaries and had become head of a school in Paris's Montparnasse quarter, the Institut de la Personnalité Créatrice. Having heard his name mentioned by people from the National Theatre School of Canada in Montreal, which he had visited briefly, Richard Fréchette and I went there together, telling ourselves that we would at least get a chance to catch a few shows in Paris.

Knapp's work was very exacting, very difficult to grasp and demanded a poetic abandon that very few people could deliver. The work of the actor–creator, as he conceived of it, was a little like squeezing a lemon to get its juice. For Richard and me, his approach corresponded exactly to what we had dreamed of, to what we wanted to do. I had always been told that I didn't commit myself enough, that I didn't know how to tell my own story, and there I was, suddenly being told the complete opposite. For Knapp, my reserve and control allowed me to act better, to tell my story better. So his workshops showed me I was on the right track, even if I still hardly knew what that track was. I had been rebuked at the Conservatoire for my reserve but, because he saw its value, Knapp was suddenly allowing me to use it.

Something that helped to clarify my understanding of the difference between energy and emotion was seeing two different versions of *Amadeus*: the end of the run of the New York production and Olivier Reichenbach's production at the Théâtre du Nouveau Monde in Montreal, and then with a few cast changes at the Trident in Quebec City. Both productions had some good elements. Shaffer wrote a good play and a good play can be adapted in many different ways. But in New York, there was a strong contrast between the actors playing Mozart and Salieri, and those who played the smaller roles. Because of the size of their roles, the latter really only made fleeting appearances on stage and, near the end of the run, they had developed a kind of reserve, a coolness in their performance. No passion, no warmth. The actors weren't putting themselves into their parts as we would normally expect. But the actor playing Mozart was extraordinary and, in contrast to his entourage, he seemed to be on fire. Suddenly, I understood the idea that in this Viennese world where everything was made of marble and people listened without passion to music, there lived these two inflamed souls, Mozart and Salieri. In Reichenbach's show, on the other hand, all the actors played well and put a lot of heart and generosity into their parts. But it was terrible for the show because you could no longer see the specific intensity and warmth of the two principal characters.

In *Needles and Opium* I truly realised what this contrast meant when specific moments in which I was very cold and very controlled in my performance moved the audience, and gave them the impression of great fervour. Erland Josephson, who is one of the great Swedish actors, cried when he first saw *Needles and Opium* in Stockholm, yet I wasn't doing anything. I wasn't crying. I had been thinking about how the telephone wire was in the wrong place, about the volume of the mike being too low, all things we were told at the Conservatoire not to do on stage. It isn't a question of emotion for me. Emotion in an actor provides him with tears, not understanding, nor a mastery of this very complex art that consists in moving the audience. An actor must find the energy that will produce an emotion in his audience, not feel it himself. This is what is poorly understood in the principle of alienation in Bertolt Brecht's work. You have to feel the actor not the character. Brechtian performance is a very distinctive style of work, in which very few actors in Quebec are versed.

In countries such as Japan, all theatre is based on reserve, on the idea that you do the least possible to say the most. Japanese theatre achieves great dramatic intensity without an emotional investment on the part of the actor, without his naming the state in which he finds himself. Theatre is like a boiling cauldron: it's more interesting to show the agitated lid than what's inside.

Emotional reserve is not merely a moral issue, it also involves having faith in understanding. I often see student shows in which the actors sob on stage and both the teachers and students seem pleased. But as a member of the audience, it does nothing for me. It feels as if things are happening only on stage. This is the approach of the school of emotion, but it doesn't work on stage. It's interesting for an actor in a workshop, but not for the audience. To create a show that's moving, what you need is not to express as much emotion as possible, but to stylise the emotion, to represent it or to symbolise it. The results are much more enduring and convincing.

PYRAMIDS AND FUNNELS

> [The audience's] reading of our work is
> beyond our control. And this is some-
> thing that stimulates me enormously: the
> work no longer belongs to me – others
> suggest how it should be transformed.
>
> Robert Lepage, in conversation with
> Philippe Soldevila in 'Impressions sur
> impressions photographiques', *Protée*,
> vol. XVII, no. 1.

Theatre takes shape in flight, when its meaning and direction escape us, when it becomes a rebellious beast that
we're unable to cage. When shows transcend their cre-
ators, that's when you have theatre. This was the case with
Trilogy. We were only in charge of the show during the
first version. Afterwards, it told its own story, it did its own
revealing.

What fascinates me most about the theatre is when the
unforeseen life of a production is allowed to emerge and
we see this independent life grow beyond us.
Unfortunately, I myself don't always allow this to happen.
Sometimes, I let myself get caught up in the game of har-
nessing a play, of controlling it. Producers want to know
increasingly early how we will stage a play, what concepts

will underlie the way it is directed. So we start putting for-
ward concepts that can be very interesting, but that
imprison the play instead of freeing it. In this way, the
ideas behind a show can become more interesting than the
show itself.

An example of this was the first version of André Jean's
À propos de la demoiselle qui pleurait, which we performed at
the Centre International de Séjour in Quebec City in
1982. The play was oddly structured and we had chosen to
focus on the intimacy of the actors' performance. In
directing it, I tried to transmit the feeling of the story
rather than its meaning or resolution. In its first version,
the play was a blank slate. In other words, it was a work
that could be interpreted in many different ways, and my
first challenge was to build everything around the principal character whom we never see. Although the narrative
remained sketchy and complex, the audience left feeling
very moved, very touched. André has a special talent for
writing neutral works or at least works that give few
instructions on how they should be performed and con-
centrate instead on how they are made.

But when we were asked to redo the play at the Trident,
we let ourselves get carried away. We were putting the
play on in a more established theatre designed for a larger
audience and trying to recreate an event out of its original
context. We became very preoccupied by what this might
mean, because we were no longer working from a clean
slate, but from the way we had filled in the blanks the first
time around. Ultimately, it was less successful because it
was produced in a very orderly and overly explained way.
If you try to structure a show too much, you can sometimes lose out in the process.

I remember an interview Françoise Faucher did with
Marguerite Duras, in which she asked the author what
point there was in writing, when, in our world of images,

each image was worth a thousand words. Duras replied that in fact it was the other way around: each word is worth a thousand images. An ideogram, a poem, a few words from a novel, a title can all suffice to inspire a show, as long as they open up on to the larger world rather than funnelling down.

I believe in the kind of theatre that starts with a single word and leads to bigger things. This is what Shakespeare did when he wrote *The Tempest*. He started with the word 'freedom', and then broadened his focus as far as he could. By the time Shakespeare reaches us, other levels have been added to this pyramid, and it is our task to enlarge it even further. Our approach to theatre, on the other hand, tends to be funnel-shaped. We bring the text back to its point of origin to show people where it came from. We treat plays like intellectual problems that need to be solved and only focus on their socio-political or intellectual value. We congratulate ourselves for finding solutions, for creating an equation that works, although sometimes to the detriment of certain parts of the text that don't fit all that well with our concept, and which we then decide to cut from the production. This is extremely annoying, in my opinion.

To continue broadening *The Tempest* we have to move beyond our focus on the word 'freedom', beyond simply showing the audience that this is the predominant theme in the work. Each scene, each character, each word has to be considered in its relation to freedom, so that we experience the liberating feeling from beginning to end and at all the different levels. The audience needs to see freedom in expression and form: the form must be the content and the content the form.

Here, in Stockholm, a friend of mine saw a version of *The Tempest* put on by a group of deaf and dumb actors. A professional actress had learned sign language to be able to work with them. My friend told me that they had taken extraordinary liberties. It was almost imperative – just try communicating Shakespeare's pentametre and seventeenth-century vocabulary in sign language. Their work was very uninhibited. They invented expressions, new ways of saying things. And so they achieved this freedom of form that the play is all about. And the form is the substance.

When we worked on *The Seven Streams of the River Ota* in London in October of 1994, it was our ideas about form that helped us develop the show. The actors would ask themselves how to perform something and then become aware that the form demanded that it be played in such a way.

Although few like to admit it, *The Dragons' Trilogy* is more than a written text; it's also a form. The direction and blocking, the *mise en scène*, is as eloquent as the text, sometimes more so. The actors' performance expresses at times the *mise en scène* rather than the text. Some works age more than others – Anouilh much more than Ionesco, for example. The same goes for productions. If the *mise en scène* of *The Dragons' Trilogy* – the show's principal defining element – doesn't hold up, we have no reason to tell the story a second time. If we were to remount it, I would restructure some elements and stage them differently, rather than simply do a revival.

Another example is *Tectonic Plates*. It was a difficult project, the cause of many disagreements and clashes before the work came together. We were frequently letting people go or putting together new teams. And Marie Gignac pointed out to me that it was the nature of the work we had chosen. We were speaking of drifting, of the impact of shifting continental plates. So it was natural that our work should reflect these things. It could be very difficult, but the rewards were equally great at the moments when it finally came together.

When we started *Tectonic Plates* we thought we had a lot of freedom, both in form and content, mostly because of *The Dragons' Trilogy*, where we had mixed very different forms and styles. But this wasn't the case. We had sung Kurt Weil's music in the middle of a show on China. We had set Tai Chi to music by Peter Gabriel and Philip Glass. The possibilities had seemed infinite. And it had all worked. It had all converged on the same point, the idea of becoming a complete being, of bringing together the Yin and the Yang.

But in *Tectonic Plates*, everything revolved around breakage and shock, around division. Things became more complex because we were no longer speaking of convergence. The ideas themselves would collide, unite and then come apart, create an extraordinary whole, then drift and break apart. This is what happened for four years. We had extraordinary meetings and enormous collisions. It was one of our great creative projects. Our flops – in Montreal, where we couldn't even perform the show at the Festival de Théâtre des Amériques – were as frequent as our triumphs – in London, for instance. But these triumphs and failures had to do with the show itself, not with the audience or the show's technical complexity or how developed the production was. One moment, everything held in place and we felt we had the show well in hand. The next moment it all fell apart, escaping us again and going off in a thousand different directions.

The shape of a show depends on its subject. *Needles and Opium* moves from image to word, as dictated by Cocteau's own text. If I developed a project on a poet or a songwriter, my main concern would be to research sound.

Vinci is a good example. Having gone to Italy and done my research on the show, I came to the conclusion that, with or without money, with or without technical means, the show had to create the impression of technical ingenuity. I didn't have precise ideas about the visual appearance of the show, only the feeling that to reveal Leonardo da Vinci's genius and his gifts as an engineer, we had to develop a show that was equally resourceful. That's how you open up what there is to say. Even if you barely scratch the surface of the infinite number of his works and writings, the show will express this resourcefulness through its form, by presenting things on the verge of flight, on water, by presenting the play of shadow and light, of chiaroscuro. Rather than naming da Vinci's obsessions, you make them come alive. That's how best to tell the story, to make da Vinci comprehensible to the audience. In theatre, the audience has to be immersed in the show's argument, and to be immersed in the argument every sense has to seize it and so the form has to become an incarnation of the subject and themes.

If we have nothing to say, the form remains simply the form, the medium the medium. But if we have something to say, the medium will be the message. I have met some remarkable men who argue this, who know this. Cocteau knew this and, as I noticed while researching *Needles*, he was criticised throughout his life for the same things as I am. He was considered an acrobat, an aesthete without substance, a formalist. But once the dust settles, you see what endures.

When Cocteau writes about opium, you can find the rhythm and movement of opium in his poetry. And the moment one reads it aloud one realises this. When I pick this theme up in *Needles and Opium*, this is the moment in the show when I am not in a harness, when Cocteau's character isn't flying. And it's also the moment when it's most easy to cast a spell on the audience with words.

And Cocteau's genius is that his writing reflects the nature of his themes: speed, translucence, childhood.

Cocteau saw – or wished to see – death through the veil of life. His poetic theories overlap with some contemporary scientific theories. For example, according to Cocteau, the reason we don't see other dimensions – the world of spirits – is because they move at a much greater speed than we do. This is where the image of a propeller came from in *Needles*. Is there anything more solid, more cutting and more opaque than a propeller? But when it turns, it becomes transparent, it seems immaterial and it no longer prevents us from seeing what's hidden behind it. But if you put your hand through it, the propeller will cut it off. This is what death is like. Here, Cocteau touched on characteristics of matter that preoccupy many scientists today.

WATCHING THE SHOW

If this idea of opening up, of theatre that 'takes shape in flight', has to do with creating theatre that is more alive, that generates more questions than answers, Robert Lepage is also concerned with a variation on this theme that has to do with the perception the audience has of a show. For him, a play is an open work largely because of the diversity of onlookers.

These days, I am constantly surprised to see how differently the actors, technicians and I all perceive the production. We are all observing the same show – whether it's *A Dream Play* or something else entirely – but we don't see the same show. We don't look at the same things. We don't have the same ideas. We have to accept this as fact. Then we can work together. It's not the performance that creates the show, nor the directing, nor the text. It's something very nebulous that makes the whole more than the sum of its parts, that results in our creating an event on the stage. It can come out of the work, of the context in which we perform the play or out of the city in which we perform it – because perceptions of theatre differ from one place to another and even from one person to another.

One member of the audience doesn't see the same things on the stage as the person sitting next to him. What differentiates theatre from film, among other things, is this idea of choice. Someone can sit in a theatre and freely choose what to look at. A theatre director doesn't make as many choices as a film director. In film, we see what the director wants us to see. He blows it up, he edits it, he makes sure that we look at what he wants us to. But in theatre, each member of the audience chooses which character to look at, and can look at what he wants, listen to what he wants, can watch one actor's performance rather than another's, or the lighting or the props. So, shifting one scene while editing a film has a much more profound impression on the overall effect of the film than shifting a scene in a play. A theatrical show must suggest a multitude of readings. Anyone who wants to read my shows only on the basis of the actors' performance risks being disappointed. And it's difficult to create shows that offer these multiple readings.

I often notice that actors who sit in on my rehearsals don't watch the show. They watch one of the actors performing. They tell me he's good, whereas I'll find his work worthless because he's out of place in the context of the show, or moving awkwardly, or his rhythm is off. Theatre is a tray filled with hors-d'oeuvres from which we can choose what we wish. We try to carry the meaning as far as possible, but what really makes plays like *The Dragons' Trilogy*, Brook's *Mahabharata* or some of Mnouchkine's shows successful is that we are offered a selection – one that's coherent, but a selection nonetheless.

We shouldn't spend our time making sure that the audience feels and thinks a certain way at a certain moment. We have to create a coherent world, a coherent environment from which the audience takes what it wants. This is not what I'm criticised for when I'm told that my shows are bad. And some of my shows are bad. That's perhaps what disappoints me most in reviews. They write that the actors aren't good, or that I'm a spoilt child playing with my toys. But they don't see that a bad show is bad because of its lack of coherence and fundamentally that has nothing to do with the choice of actors or the use of technology.

It's with the aim of creating an inclusive and coherent environment that, before working on a play in rehearsal, I also give a lot of time to the set, to lighting, to costumes. Directors often work at great length on the text and then invite the set designer or costume maker, for example, to illustrate the general concept they've developed. I try not to push my ideas too much, so that I don't cripple the other artists. They come with their own notions about what light to shed on the play, and this allows us to exchange ideas and allows me to make suggestions that carry some ideas further. It's a bit back to front, but I think it helps let the play speak without being too sharply forced in one direction. I don't make any decisions in rereading the text on the morning of the first rehearsal. I take notes, I feel things, but mostly I draw on what comes up during the rehearsal.

Directing isn't the sole property of the director. With our approach, it comes out of a collective effort. When we rehearse with actors, we discover and uncover the play. When I direct, my approach is closer to that of a student than that of a teacher. I think this is what makes the play continue to evolve right until opening night and even beyond it.

We ask the play to teach us, to show us what it holds.

For most directors, the work is done in a funnel. They start with tons of ideas that they bring down to a general principle, towards an intended destination, as a way to help order the play. This kind of approach is reassuring for actors, who then only have to execute the director's orders. I think there's a difference here between North America and Europe. Europe has a master/student culture, especially in places like Germany and Russia, where people want to be told how to think and the actors grant a certain credibility to the director because of who he is and because of his reputation. In Munich, it took a long time before they were able to feel comfortable with our method of working, and it was a while before the actors started to enjoy working our way. And when they finally did, Philippe Soldevila and I thought, 'Great, but now we have to leave.' At times, the culture clash between these approaches can be considerable.

Personally, I prefer to start with a single idea – the passing of time in *A Dream Play*, for example – and from there to broaden my focus. And the more we work on it, the more the play opens up. Rather than rummaging through every corner in order to offer the actors a definitive idea of the play, I try to plant the right seed at the start.

END

ECHOES OF ELSINORE

Just as a book's preface is the last section to be written, it seemed logical that our conversations should end on a discussion of the birth of a show. On 9 June 1995, Robert Lepage and I began discussing a new topic, aspects of which had periodically filtered into our conversations over the previous nine months: a new one-man show, planned for September 1995, called Elsinore, *named after the castle in which Hamlet, Prince of Denmark, spoke his famous soliloquies. It is not my intention here to give an account of this show [which has since been performed and toured the world during 1996]. The tendency of Robert Lepage's shows to be in perpetual evolution would, at any rate, make this an impossible task. But, keeping to the idea of the travel log that governs this book's structure, we wanted to follow the trail of his creative process and record the first steps on a path whose destination was still unknown.*

How much of what is said here still applies to Elsinore *in its state? Were the stated objectives fulfilled? Do the themes originally put forth still make sense in the production? With the amount of change which can take place at any time in Robert Lepage's shows, these remain completely open-ended questions.*

I've always dreamed of doing a work that is more auditory than visual, a work that is really text-based. This was part of the frustration I experienced with *Needles and Opium*. I wanted to include Cocteau's *Lettre aux Américains* in its entirety, a work that is unfortunately not theatrical enough. There was a lot of text work in *Needles*, which I liked a great deal and which this new project allows me to carry much farther because it's based on *Hamlet*.

There's obviously a whole host of reasons to be interested in *Hamlet*, a masterpiece of world theatre pulsing with a thousand and one themes. The instructions Hamlet gives to the actors in the third act particularly speak to me. I find a lot of my own ideas about theatre in his words: 'Do not saw the air too much with your hand, thus, but use all gently; for in the very torrent, tempest, and, as I may say, whirlwind of your passion, you must acquire and beget a temperance that may give it smoothness', or again 'for anything so o'erdone is from the purpose of playing'.

All the same, the theme that speaks to me most – especially in the context of a one-man show – is the incestuous nature of the relationships between the characters. The impetus of the play is that Hamlet's mother's marriage to his father's brother is considered incestuous. The word incest here is used not only in the strictest sense. It also refers to the extreme closeness of the characters, who are defined by their relationships to one another. For me, this theme – which plays an important role in *The Confessional* – also makes us question the incestuous nature of society as a whole, or of certain milieux. We have only to think of how many times we in Quebec use this term to describe the theatre world or world of the arts in general.

With this in mind, the blood ties that link Hamlet, Gertrude, Hamlet's father and his uncle Claudius make it possible for us to imagine a single actor playing all the roles in the family. Another actor could, in the same way, play the other family, made up of Polonius, Laertes and Ophelia. And when Hamlet declares that Laertes is his mirror – so that Laertes, his opposite, reacts in an exaggerated manner when Hamlet remains paralysed – we can even go so far as to unite both families in a single actor. This is why the show is called *Elsinore*. It's not just about

Hamlet. It also assembles in a single person all the aspects of the universe of Elsinore.

Besides this notion of assembling and my interest in the text, the death of my own father in 1992 also renewed my longstanding interest in *Hamlet*. I found myself, in a certain way, haunted by the ghost of my own father, and I was called to question my relationship with my mother, my brother, heredity, and so on. My one-man shows often deal with the loss of a loved one – the suicide of a friend in *Vinci*, the loss of a lover in *Needles and Opium*. So the idea of dealing with the death of a father here seemed to fit into a recurring pattern. The context naturally threw me into Shakespeare's play.

At the start of 1993, a few weeks after beginning the project, I met Bob Wilson by chance over breakfast in Toronto and he told me that he was planning to direct *Hamlet* as a one-man show. Like me, he intended to play all the characters, and his show was due to go on only a few months before mine. And then, during a meeting I had with Peter Brook in Munich, he told me that he was also interested in *Hamlet*, especially the whole question of translation. Given their projects, I suddenly found myself in an awkward situation and I put my *Hamlet* on ice to start working on another project based on language and the musicality of language – a one-man show revolving around the French writer/songwriter Serge Gainsbourg's *L'homme à la tête de chou*.

I set to work with Robert Caux and we developed a whole method of working on the text, and kept at it for several months. But ultimately, we had to concede to the obvious. Try as we might to work on *L'homme à la tête de chou*, we always seemed to come back to *Hamlet*. After consulting those closest to me, I finally decided to take it up again, without, however, abandoning the Gainsbourg project, which I'd very much like to return to in a limited context.[7] This detour had nonetheless enriched my work on *Hamlet*: first, because the cold and intelligent passion that Gainsbourg constantly breathes into the dramas of his songs is the same passion that Hamlet speaks of to the actors; and also because one of Shakespeare's great strengths lies in his play with words and the experiment with sound in his writing. We tried to keep this in mind when we worked on the French text, based on François-Victor Hugo's translation.

The text's musicality is an essential element of Shakespeare's writing. In the first folio edition of *Hamlet*, there are many sound cues, telling us which syllables to accentuate and how to balance the iambic pentameter. What opera reveals to me – the way the subtext can be found in the music – also exists in the rhythm and song of Shakespeare's writing.

In my work with Robert Caux, we try to 'X-ray' the text, as it were, to capture its inherent musicality. We work with a machine that recognises different types of pronounced syllables and that associates a particular musical sound with each one. When we put Hamlet through this filter, its meaning emerged in a whole new way. When Hamlet meets the ghost of his father, for example, the latter says, 'I am thy father's spirit, Doom'd for a certain term to walk the night, And for the day confin'd to fast in fires.' The accent is placed on the 'f's and 's's, which creates a precise kind of music that's different, say, from another segment of the text in which the 'p's and 'r's are brought to the fore. If you use this method to filter the ghost's words, 'a serpent stung me', you can really hear the serpent's hiss in the text.

Given that we were working simultaneously on an English and a French version of the show, our whole approach obviously brought questions of translation to the forefront. If the musicality of each language is different, the music of the text will necessarily be transformed in the translation. Preserving the meaning of the play becomes a very important part of the process.

This sound work doesn't exclude an equal focus on visual devices. Rosencrantz and Guildenstern, for example, are not among the characters played by the single actor. So, here we replace them with two surveillance cameras. They are located at the two extremities of the stage and focused on the actor. The cameras help to highlight the role of both these characters as spies, as well as the whole recurring motif of espionage and surveillance. So not only does the audience see the actor live but from two other points of view, which change, depending on whether the actor distances himself from or approaches Rosencrantz or Guildenstern.

The sound work, which makes both music and text the central focus of the show, remains our principal means of filtering *Hamlet* through technology. It also gives the show a fluidity and changeability. The music emitted by the machine in direct response to the text is modified according to each night's performance. In this way, each night the show will be able to undergo small transformations, and never be exactly the same . . .

THE BEGINNING OF THE END

Most of the time, a theatrical production is constructed in the following order: writing, rehearsal, performance and, sometimes, translation. I've noticed over time that in our creations, the process is, in a sense, reversed: the real writing happens at the end. Our creative work begins with a huge brain-storming and a collective drawing session where ideas are grouped together. Then, we discuss ideas that have been singled out, which leads us to improvisation. Then there's the phase of structuring the improvisations, which we rehearse, and eventually perform publicly. These performances, rather than being the culmination of the process, are really further rehearsals for us, since the show is not written down or fixed. Because we perform our plays in a number of countries, the translation is done at about this stage. For *The Seven Streams of the River Ota*, we rehearsed in French and in English, and a part of the text was adapted for a German audience during rehearsals for the shows in Vienna and Braunschweig in the summer of 1995. To my mind, the text for a show can't be written down until all these stages have taken place, when all the performances are over. It's only at this point that the shape and the subject matter have stopped evolving.

If you look at this process in cyclical terms, it means that the cycles in which I work are out of step with the conventional sequence. Simply put, writing-rehearsal-performance-translation becomes rehearsal-performance-translation-writing. Seen in a linear manner, the starting point for most creations becomes, for me, their final point.

PROFESSIONAL CHRONOLOGY

1978 – Graduated from the Conservatoire d'Art
Dramatique de Québec. Did a three-week
workshop with Alain Knapp in Paris. Founded
Théâtre Hummm... with Richard Fréchette.

1979 – *L'attaque quotidienne*, written by Robert Lepage
and Richard Fréchette, produced by Théâtre
Hummm... (Quebec City). First performed at Le
Bar Zinc in Quebec City.

Directed *Arlequin, serviteur de deux maîtres* by Carlo
Goldoni, with Richard Fréchette at Collège
Lévis-Lauzon . Won best prize at the Cap-Rouge
Student Theatre Festival.

Directed *La ferme des animaux*, adapted from
George Orwell's *Animal Farm* by Paule Fillion,
Michèle Laperrière, Robert Lepage and Suzanne
Poliquin, produced by Théâtre Hummm...
(Quebec City). First performed at the Centre
François-Charron in Quebec City and invited to
the Festival de l'Association Québécoise de Jeune
Théâtre.

1980 – *Saturday Night Taxi*, a collective by Richard
Fréchette, Francine Lafontaine and Robert
Lepage, produced by Théâtre Hummm... First

performed at the Centre François-Charron, remounted at the café-théâtre Le Hobbit in the spring of 1981.

Directed *Oomeragh ooh!* by Jean Truss, produced by Marionnettes du Grand Théâtre (Quebec City). First performed at the Grand Théâtre de Québec.

Directed *L'école, c'est secondaire*, a collective by Denis Bernard, Michel Nadeau and Camil Bergeron, produced by Théâtre Repère. Toured high schools in Greater Quebec City.

1981 – Directed *Dix petits nègres*, adapted from *Ten Little Niggers* by Agatha Christie at collège Lévis-Lauzon.

Directed *Le coq*, adapted from *La zizanie* by Albert Uderzo and René Goscinny, produced by the Méchatigan Troupe (Sainte-Marie-de-Beauce).

Acted in *Les Américanoïaques* by Rezvani, directed by Gaston Hubert, produced by and performed at Théâtre de la Bordée (Quebec City).

Directed *Jour de pluie* by Gérard Bibeau, produced by the Marionnettes du Grand Théâtre de Québec.

1982 – Directed *Pas d'chicane dans ma cabane*, a collective work by Michel Bernatchez, Odile Pelletier and Marco Poulin, produced by Théâtre d'Bon'Humeur (Quebec City). First performed at the Centre François-Charron.

Joined Théâtre Repère with Richard Fréchette.

Directed a scene in *Claudico bric-à-brac* by Luc Simard, produced by the Marionnettes du Grand Théâtre. First performed at the Grand Théâtre de Québec.

Directed *En attendant*, a collective work by Richard Fréchette, Robert Lepage and Jacques Lessard, produced by Théâtre Repère. First performed at the café-théâtre Le Hobbit.

Directed *Les rois mangent*, a collective work by Théâtre d'Bon'Humeur. First performed at the Centre François-Charron and also performed at Théâtre de la Bordée.

Directed *À demi-lune*, a collective work by Johanne Bolduc, Estelle Dutil and Robert Lepage, produced by Théâtre Repère. First performed at l'Anglicane in Lévis.

1983 – Directed *Dieu et l'amour complexe*, collage of texts by Woody Allen, at the Conservatoire d'Art Dramatique de Québec.

Directed *Coriolan et le monstre aux mille têtes*, adapted from William Shakespeare, produced by Théâtre Repère. First performed at Théâtre de la Bordée.

Directed *Carmen*, adapted from Georges Bizet's opera, produced by Théâtre d'Bon'Humeur. Performed at Théâtre de la Bordée.

Actor-Puppeteer in *À vol d'oiseau* by André Jean, directed by Gérard Bibeau, produced by Marionnettes du Grand Théâtre. First performed at the Grand Théâtre de Québec.

The beginning of *Top Repère* evenings, a series of
sketches, improvisations and acts performed on
Monday nights as part of Théâtre de la Bordée's
1983–4 season and in the autumn of 1984. The
evenings had approximately thirty creative
contributors, Lepage among them.

1984 – Directed *Solange passe*, by Jocelyne Corbeil and
Lucie Godbout, produced by and performed at
Théâtre de la Bordée.

Directed *Circulations*, a collective work by
François Beausoleil, Bernard Bonnier, Lise
Castonguay and Robert Lepage, produced by
Théâtre Repère. First performed at Théâtre de la
Bordée. Toured in Rimouski, Chicoutimi,
Jonquière, Lévis, Quebec City, Montreal,
Ottawa, Toronto, Sudbury, Winnipeg,
Edmonton, Vancouver. Won the Grand Prix at
the Quinzaine Internationale de Théâtre de
Québec.

Directed *Stand-by 5 minutes*, a collective work by
Jean-Jacqui Boutet, Louis-Georges Girard,
Ginette Guay, Martine Ouellet and Marie St-Cyr,
produced by Théâtre de la Bordée in
collaboration with Théâtre de l'Equinoxe
(Quebec City). Performed at Théâtre de la
Bordée, remounted at Théâtre Paul-Hébert the
following season.

Acted in the television series *Court-circuit*,
produced by Radio-Canada.

Won the O'Keefe Trophy for the actor awarded
the most stars, and the Pierre-Curzi Trophy for

the recruit of the year at the Ligue Nationale d'Improvisation.

1985 – Directed *À propos de la demoiselle qui pleurait*, by André Jean, produced by Théâtre Repère. First performed at the Centre International de Séjour de Québec. A new version performed at Théâtre du Trident in Quebec City in January 1986.

Created, directed, acted *Comment regarder le point de fuite*, a one-man show, produced by Théâtre Repère. First performed at the Implanthéâtre, and in the first part of *Point de fuite*, a multidisciplinary show in which Robert Lepage also acted.

Directed *Histoires sorties du tiroir*, by Gérard Bibeau, produced by the Marionnettes du Grand Théâtre. First performed at the Grand Théâtre de Québec.

Directed *Coup de poudre*, a collective by Josée Deschênes, Martin Dion, Simon Fortin, Benoît Gouin, Hélène Leclerc, produced by Théâtre Artéfact (Quebec City) and Parks Canada. First performed at the Parc de l'Artillerie de Québec.

Acted eight roles (four men and four women) in *Comédie policière*, by Javier Arroyuelo and Rafael Lopez-Sanchez, directed by Matieu Gaumond, produced by Théâtre du Vieux-Québec. Performed at the Implanthéâtre.

Directed *California Suite*, produced by Théâtre du Bois de Coulonge (Sillery). Performed at Théâtre du Vieux Port de Québec.

Directed *The Dragons' Trilogy*, written by Marie Brassard, Jean Casault, Lorraine Côté, Marie

Gignac, Robert Lepage and Marie Michaud, produced by Théâtre Repère (first and second phases) and by the Festival de Théâtre des Amériques (third phase). First phase first performed in November 1985 at the Implanthéâtre in Quebec City. Second phase first performed in May 1986 at the Implanthéâtre. Third phase first performed in June 1987 at the Festival de Théâtre des Amériques in Montreal. Toured throughout 1986–91 in Toronto (twice), Montreal (three times), Ottawa, Quebec City (twice), Winnipeg, New York, Chicago, Boston, Knoxville (Tennessee), Los Angeles, Helena (Montana), London (twice), Galway, Adelaide, Limoges, Brussels, Wroclaw and Czestochowa (Poland), Paris, Amsterdam, Hamburg, Barcelona, Mexico City, Basel, Glasgow, Copenhagen, Milan. Won the Prix de la Fondation du Trident for best director (1986); the Grand Prix of the Festival de Théâtre des Amériques (1987); the Association Québécoise des Critiques de Théâtre's Best Show of the Year Award (1987); the Ottawa Critics' Circle Best Show of the Year Award (1987); *La Presse*'s Prix du Public and Best Show of the Year Award (1988); the Dora Mavor Moore Award for best production, Toronto Theatre Alliance (1989); Dora Mavor Moore Award for Best Set Design, Toronto Theatre Alliance (1989); Best Production Award at the Gran Festival de la Ciudad de Mexico (1990); chosen as one of the ten best shows of the year by the *Chicago Tribune* (1990).

1986 – Created, directed, acted, *Vinci*, one-man show, co-produced by Théâtre de Quat'Sous (Montreal) and Théâtre Repère. First performed at Théâtre de Quat'Sous. Toured in Montreal, Quebec City, Chicoutimi, Trois-Rivières, Sherbrooke, Rivière-du-Loup, Rimouski, Ottawa, Laval, La Pocatière, Baie-Comeau, Granby, Drummondville, Rouyn, Val d'Or, Toronto, Calgary, Paris, Avignon, Limoges, Rennes, London, Nyon. Won Best Production of the Year Award from the Association Québécoise des Critiques de Théâtre (1986); Best production at the Festival de Nyon (1987), Prix Coup de Pouce at the 'Off' Festival in Avignon (1987).

Co-directed (with Michel Nadeau) *Le bord extrème*, adapted from Ingmar Bergman's *The Seventh Seal*, produced by Théâtre Repère. First performed at the Implanthéâtre.

Directed *Comment être parfait en trois jours* by Gilles Gauthier, adapted from *Be a Perfect Person in Just Three Days* by Stephen Manes, produced by Théâtre des Confettis (Quebec City). First performed at the Implanthéâtre and on tour since 1986 (performed more than 500 times).

Co-Artistic Director with Jacques Lessard of Théâtre Repère (until 1989).

Directed one scene in the comedy show *Le Groupe Sanguin: Prise I*, produced by the Groupe Sanguin (Montreal). Toured throughout the province of Quebec.

Won the Prix de Création from the Conseil de la Culture de Québec.

1987 – Directed *Polygraph* by Robert Lepage and Marie Brassard, produced by Théâtre Repère, with Cultural Industry and the Almeida Theatre, London. First performed at the Implanthéâtre. Toured and touring in Montreal, Quebec City, Toronto, New York, London, Amsterdam, Nuremberg, Maubeuge, Barcelona, Hamburg, Ottawa, Belgium, the Netherlands, Scotland, France, Hong Kong . . . Japanese version created in Tokyo, 1996. Won the Chalmers' Award for Best Canadian Play, Toronto (1991); Best Production, *Time Out* magazine, London (1989).

Directed *En pleine nuit une sirène* by Jacques Girard and Robert Lepage, produced by and first performed at Théâtre de la Bordée.

Lighting for *Danses-tu?*, a collective work, produced by Théâtre Niveau Parking (Quebec City). First performed at the Après-Onze Bar and then at the Implanthéâtre.

Directed the comedy show *Le Groupe Sanguin: Prise II*, produced by the Groupe Sanguin (Montreal). Toured throughout the province of Quebec.

Directed *Pour en finir une fois pour toutes avec Carmen*, freely adapted from Georges Bizet's opera, produced by Théâtre de Quat'Sous in Montreal. Remounted at the Institut Canadien in Quebec City, 1988.

Acted the role of Nero in *Les Grands Esprits*, produced by Radio-Canada.

Won the Prix Metro-Star for the Québécois artist who has enjoyed most success abroad.

1988 – Directed *Tectonic Plates*, produced by Théâtre Repère and Cultural Industry, with Festival de Théâtre des Amériques, Glasgow 1990, Channel 4 television and the Royal National Theatre. First performed at the Du Maurier World Stage Festival in Toronto. Toured in Montreal, Quebec City, Toronto, London, Glasgow, Barcelona.

Directed *Songe d'une nuit d'été*, by William Shakespeare at Théâtre du Nouveau Monde (Montreal). Won the Prix Gascon-Roux for best director (1988). New box-office record at the Théâtre du Nouveau Monde.

Directed a commercial advertisement for the Syndicat de la fonction publique du Québec. Won Best Production Award from the Publicité Club de Montréal.

Directed a commercial advertisement for Loto-Québec.

Acted role of Pontius Pilate in *Jesus of Montreal*, feature film by Denys Arcand, produced by Max Films.

Won Prix Gémeaux for Best Television Performance in *La soirée de l'impro* – Ligue nationale d'improvisation.

1989 – Appointed Artistic Director of French Theatre at the National Arts Centre in Ottawa, a position he held until May 1993. Left Théâtre Repère.

Directed *La vie de Galilée* by Bertolt Brecht, produced by and first performed at Théâtre du Nouveau Monde. Won Prix Gascon-Roux for

Best Director (1989). Another new record for ticket sales at the TNM.

Co-director of a bilingual production of *Romeo and Juliet*, by William Shakespeare, co-produced by Théâtre Repère and Night Cap Productions (Saskatoon). First performed in Saskatoon. Toured in Stratford, Ottawa, Toronto, Sudbury.

Directed *Echo*, adapted from *A Nun's Diary* by Ann Diamond, produced by Théâtre 1774 (Montréal) and Théâtre Passe-Muraille (Toronto). First performed at the Saydie Bronfman Centre (Montreal). Remounted in Toronto in 1990.

Directed *Mère Courage et ses enfants*, by Bertolt Brecht at the Conservatoire d'Art Dramatique (Quebec City).

Collaborated on *C'est ce soir qu'on saoûle Sophie Saucier*, by Sylvie Provost, with Les Productions Ma Chère Pauline (Montreal).

1990 – Directed *La Visite de la Vieille Dame*, by Friedrich Dürenmatt, produced by the National Arts Centre in Ottawa. Remounted at the Salle Albert Rousseau (Quebec City).

1991 – Created, directed, acted in *Needles and Opium*, one-man show, produced by Productions d'Albert (Quebec City), the National Arts Centre and Productions AJP (Montreal). First performed at the Palais Montcalm in Quebec City. Toured and touring in Montreal, Ottawa, New York, Frankfurt, Munich, Maubeuge, London, Florence, Barcelona, Paris, Stockholm (last performance by Robert Lepage in Stockholm, 18

September 1994 – replaced by Marc Labrèche),
Basle, Budapest, Arnhem, Leiden, Enschede,
Haarlem, Hasselt, Turnhout, Neerpelt, Chalon-
sur-Saône, Rungis, Chicoutimi, Amos, Baie-
Comeau, Montreal, Vancouver, Zurich, Glasgow,
Roanne, Saint-Etienne, Chambéry, Valence,
Privas, Meylan, Villeurbanne, Nagoya, Gatineau,
Saint Louis . . . Won the Chalmers' Award for
Best Canadian Play (1995). New version by
Italian producer, Segriali, featuring Argentinian
actor, Nestor Saied. Touring in Spain and Italy in
the fall of 1997.

Directed *Los Cincos Soles*, an acting exercise with
graduates of the National Theatre School in
Montreal. Performed at the National Arts Centre.

1992 – Directed *Alanienouidet*, by Marianne Ackerman
and Robert Lepage at the National Arts Centre.
Remounted at the Carrefour International de
Théâtre in Quebec City.

Directed *La Tempête*, by William Shakespeare at
the National Arts Centre Atelier as part of
ARTO, the Atelier de Recherche Théâtrale de
l'Outaouais.

Directed *Macbeth*, by William Shakespeare at the
University of Toronto.

Directed *Bluebeard's Castle*, by Béla Bartók, and
Ewartung, by Arnold Schoenberg, co-produced by
the Canadian Opera Company (Toronto) and the
Brooklyn Academy of Music (New York).
Toured in Edinburgh, New York, Melbourne.
Remounted in Toronto, Geneva, Jerusalem . . .
Won the Edinburgh International Critics' Award

(1993) and *Scotsman*'s Hamada Festival Prize (1993).

Directed *A Midsummer Night's Dream* by William Shakespeare, produced by the National Theatre (London). Robert Lepage was the first Canadian to direct a Shakespeare play at the National.

Subject of *Who's that nobody from Quebec?*, documentary on Robert Lepage, produced by Hauer Rawlence (London) and the British Broadcasting Corporation.

Directed the Shakespeare Cycle (*Coriolan, Macbeth, La Tempête*), translated by Michel Garneau, co-produced by Théâtre Repère, Manège (Maubeuge, France), the Am Turm Theatre (Frankfurt) and the Festival d'Automne (Paris). First performed in Maubeuge. Toured (1992–1994) in Paris, Frankfurt, Zurich, Basle, Amsterdam, Chalon-sur-Saône, Hamburg, Nottingham (*Coriolan*), Montreal, Tokyo, Quebec City.

Played himself in *Desperanto or Let Sleeping Girls Lie*, skit directed by Patricia Rozema in *Montréal vu par . . .*, produced by Cinémaginaire (Montreal), Atlantis Films (Toronto), in association with the National Film Board of Canada.

Acted in *Ding et Dong: le Film* by Alain Chartrand, produced by Max Films.

1993 – Directed and designed Peter Gabriel's *Secret World Tour*, produced by Real World Tours Ltd (Box, United Kingdom). Toured in 1993 – more than

one hundred shows in nineteen countries
(Sweden, Norway, Germany, Switzerland,
France, Belgium, the Netherlands, Spain, Italy,
the United Kingdom, Ireland, the United States,
Canada, Turkey, Mexico, Chile, Argentina,
Brazil, Venezuela); in 1994 (partial use of the
stage design), thirty-nine shows in fifteen
countries (India, Australia, Japan, Hong Kong,
Germany, Egypt, Israel, Slovakia, Austria,
Norway, Denmark, Belgium, the Netherlands,
Switzerland, the United States).

Directed *National Capitale Nationale* by Vivienne
Laxdal and Jean-Marc Dalpé, produced by the
National Arts Centre. First performed at the
National Arts Centre Studio.

Directed *Map of Dreams*, collage of texts about
dreams by William Shakespeare, produced by and
performed at the Bayerisches Staatsschauspielhaus
(Munich).

Directed *Macbeth* and *The Tempest* in Japanese
translation at the Globe Theatre (Tokyo)

1994 – Founding Artistic Director of Ex Machina,
multidisciplinary production company based in
Quebec City.

Filming of *The Confessional* in Quebec City and
Montreal, editing in Paris, produced by
Cinémaginaire (Montreal), Enigma Films
(London) and Cinéa (France).

Directed first phase of *The Seven Streams of the
River Ota*, a collective work by Eric Bernier,
Normand Bissonnette, Rebecca Blankenship,

Anne-Marie Cadieux, Normand Daneau, Richard Fréchette, Marie Gignac, Robert Lepage and Ghislaine Vincent. Produced by Ex Machina (Quebec City) and Cultural Industry (London) with Edinburgh International Festival, Manchester City of Drama, Wiener Festwochen, Maison des Arts de Créteil, Beck's at Meadowbank (Edinburgh), Tramway (Glasgow), Upper Camfield Market (Manchester), Riverside (London). First performed at the Edinburgh International Festival in August 1994. Toured in Glasgow, Manchester, London, Paris.

Directed *Ett Drömspel* (*A Dream Play*) by August Strindberg, produced by the Kungliga Dramatiska Teatern (Stockholm). Performed at the Dramaten. Remounted in Glasgow in the spring of 1995.

Directed *Noises, Sounds and Sweet Airs*, opera by Michael Nyman, based on *The Tempest* by William Shakespeare, co-produced by the Globe Theatre (Tokyo) and the Shin-Kobe Oriental Theatre (Tokyo). First performed at the Globe Theatre.

Awarded the National Arts Centre Special Award of the Governor-General's Award for the Performing Arts.

1995 – Première of *The Confessional* at the opening of the Quinzaine des Réalisateurs at the Cannes Film Festival, produced by Cinémaginaire. Opening film at the Toronto International Film Festival. Featured at international festivals in Vancouver, Namur, Blois, London, Baie-Comeau, Istanbul,

and at Montreal's Rendez-vous du Cinéma
Québecois. Won the Rogers Award for Best
Canadian Screenplay, Vancouver (1995); the Prix
de la meilleure contribution artistique, Namur
(1995); the Genie Awards for Best Movie, Best
Directing, Best Artistic Direction, and the Prix
Claude-Jutra for the Best First Feature Film,
Montreal (1995); the International Critics Award,
Istanbul (1996); selected to represent Canada at
the Golden Globe Awards and at the Academy
Awards (1996).

Member of the Order of Canada.

Member of the Ordre de la Pléiade.

Directed second phase of *The Seven Streams of the
River Ota*, a collective work by Eric Bernier,
Normand Bissonnette, Rebecca Blankenship,
Marie Brassard, Anne-Marie Cadieux, Normand
Daneau, Richard Fréchette, Marie Gignac,
Patrick Goyette, Robert Lepage and Ghislaine
Vincent. Public rehearsals in Quebec City in
February and April. First performed at the Wiener
Festwochen, June 1995 (Vienna). Produced by Ex
Machina and Cultural Industry, with the
Edinburgh Arts Festival, Manchester 94 City of
Drama, la Maison des Arts de Créteil, the Wiener
Festwochen, les Productions d'Albert (Sainte-
Foy), le Centre Culturel de Drummondville, le
Centre Culturel de l'Université de Sherbrooke,
les Productions Specta (Trois-Rivières),
Theaterformen 95 (Braunschweig, Germany),
Change Performing Arts (Milan), IMBE
Barcelona, Präsidialabteilung der Städt
Zürich/Züricher Theater Spektakel, the Aarhus

Festuge (Denmark), Bunkamura Tokyo, Harbourfront Centre (Toronto) and the Kampnagel Hamburg. Toured in Vienna, Braunschweig, Spoleto, Barcelona, Zurich, Aarhus, Tokyo, Toronto, Hamburg.

Created, directed, acted in *Elsinore*, one-man show based on *Hamlet* by William Shakespeare. Sound and music by Robert Caux, produced by Ex Machina with the Musée d'Art Contemporain (Montreal), Productions d'Albert (Sainte-Foy), le Centre Culturel de Drummondville, le Centre Culturel de l'Université de Sherbrooke, les Productions Specta (Trois-Rivières), le Manège (Maubeuge, France), Hebbel Theatre (Berlin), Schouwenburg Theatre (Rotterdam), la Maison des Arts de Créteil, Cultural Industry (London), Edinburgh International Festival. First performed in Montreal, September 1995. Toured in Montreal, Quebec City, Sherbrooke, Chicago, Trois-Rivières, Maubeuge, Créteil, Toronto, Berlin, Brussels, Helsinki, Gothenburg, Oslo, Aarhus, Hamburg, Rotterdam, Limoges, Palermo, Udine, Nottingham, Newcastle, Glasgow, Cambridge, London. With British actor, Peter Darling: Ottawa, New York, Dublin, Madrid.

Directed *Songe d'une nuit d'été* (*A Midsummer Night's Dream*), William Shakespeare, (translated by Normand Chaurette), produced by Théâtre du Trident (Quebec City). Performed at the Grand Théâtre de Québec. Established a record for ticket sales.

1996 – Directed third phase of *The Seven Streams of the River Ota*. First performed at the Carrefour International de Théâtre de Québec (Quebec City). Toured in Vienna, Dresden, Copenhagen, Ludwigsburg, London, Stockholm, Paris, New York, Chicago, Montreal . . . Television adaptation (seven times seven minutes) directed by Francis Leclerc for In Extremis Images. Premiered at the Festival du nouveau cinéma et des nouveaux médias, Montreal, June 1997.

Filming of *Polygraph*, adapted from the stageplay by Robert Lepage and Marie Brassard with Michael Mackenzie, produced by In Extremis Images with Cinéa and Road Movies. Released: autumn of 1996.

1997 – Official opening of La Caserne, a multimedia production centre located in Quebec City, which has become headquarters for Ex Machina since December 1996.

Future projects include a new version of Shakespeare's *Tempest* produced by Ex Machina for Quebec City's Trident theatre and Ottawa's National Arts Centre for the spring of 1998; a stage version of Mahler's *Kindertotenlieder*, co-produced by Ex Machina and Cultural Industry, set to premiere at London's Lyric Hammersmith in May 1998; a production of *Celestina* by Ferdinando de Rojas, co-produced by Ex Machina and Kungliga Dramatiska Teatern, to be shown in Stockholm in August 1998 as part of the European Capital of Culture event; *The Geometry of Miracles*, a collective work about the life and work of American architect Frank Lloyd Wright;

a television adaptation of *The Dragons' Trilogy*; *Le Pont de Québec*, a historical mini-series for television; a production of *La Damnation de Faust* by Hector Berlioz at the Saito Kinan Festival of Matsumoto, Japan, with the musical direction of Seiji Ozawa, September 1999.

NOTES

[1] Besides being the name of the company Robert Lepage worked with in the 1980s, REPÈRE is an acronym for *Ressource, Partition, Evaluation, Représentation*, the defining parts of a creative 'method' inspired by the RSVP cycles conceived by Californian architect Lawrence Halprin in 1969. Basic ideas in this method are that the process is cyclical, implying that a show is constantly a work-in-progress, and that the work should take its roots in concrete resources rather than in abstract concepts and ideas. The word *repère* means a reference point, a land-mark; *repérer* is to discover, to locate.

[2] In the first stages of the show's development, Pierre Lamontagne was a student of calligraphy who came to Japan to develop his technique. In the course of 1995, his field of study switched to *buto*, and his role in the show became more limited until finally, in the spring of 1996, it became so minor that the character was actually renamed Pierre Maltais. However, the character's function as a link between Western audiences and Japanese culture remains.

[3] Translated from Michel Coulombe, *Denys Arcand: la vraie nature du cinéaste*, Boréal, Montreal, 1993, p. 120.

[4] Howard Gardner, *Creating Minds: An Anatomy of Creativity Seen Through the Lives of Freud, Einstein, Picasso, Stravinsky, Eliot, Graham and Gandhi*, Basic Books, New York, 1993.

[5] In numerology, each letter of the alphabet corresponds to

a number (a = 1, b = 2, c = 3, etc.). To calculate Lepage's numerological number, Peter Gabriel would have added together the numbers corresponding to each letter of his name. When the total is more than a single digit, each digit is then added to the next, until a single digit remains.

[6] In the 30 June 1994 edition of *Voir*, Georges Privet wrote in his column, 'Prise de Vue': '*The Confessional* is also being talked about a great deal because it revolves around the filming of *I Confess* – which Alfred Hitchcock shot in Quebec City in 1953. And this is where the shoe pinches . . . Lepage's film leads me to question what we might call the "cultural alibi": an increasingly popular practice that tries to create an event by pirating a work that already exists.'

[7] Robert Wilson's show, *Hamlet, a Monologue*, was first presented in July 1995 in New York's Serious Fun Festival. Seeing it, Robert Lepage was able to observe just how different Wilson's approach was from his own. Any remaining fear Lepage might have had of a comparison between the two shows was also alleviated by the news that Robert Wilson had been invited by a German opera house to direct the two operas *Ewartung* and *Bluebeard's Castle* in the autumn of 1995, operas that Lepage had himself directed in 1992 for the Canadian Opera Company and which had earned him two prizes at the 1993 Edinburgh Festival. Meanwhile, Peter Brook's approach towards *Hamlet* has led him to a show called *Qui est là* ('*Who's there*' translated, literally), where excerpts of the Shakespearean text crisscross with the writings of Brecht, Meyerhold, Gordon Craig and Zeami; an approach quite distant from the solo, highly technological show conceived by Lepage.